HALLOWED GROUND

Evening on the battlefield with the Fourth New York Cavalry monument on the left and the Eighth Pennsylvania monument on the right.

THE ILLUSTRATED EDITION

HALLOWED GROUND

A WALK AT
GETTYSBURG

JAMES M. MCPHERSON
Pulitzer Prize-winning author of *Battle Cry for Freedom*

This artistic rendition of the fighting at Gettysburg may represent Pickett's Charge.

CONTENTS

A rural road into Gettysburg.

INTRODUCTION

PUBLISHED TWELVE years ago, the original edition of *Hallowed Ground* portrayed the Gettysburg battlefield and what happened there on the first three days of July 1863 in words. This new, richly illustrated edition contains those same words, but they are now supplemented by contemporary and modern photographs—many of the latter in color—contemporary illustrations, excerpts from official battle reports and other first-hand accounts, and additional visual material including several full-color maps.

The old adage that a picture is worth a thousand words may not be literally true. It nevertheless expresses an essential truth. The illustrations in this edition of *Hallowed Ground* will greatly enhance the reader's understanding and appreciation of the battle and its significance. Those who have carried the original edition around the battlefield as a guide to the various sites of action (as many have done) can now carry this illustrated edition to enrich their experiences with the additional dimension of photographs and paintings that show the battlefield as it existed in 1863 (or soon afterward), compared to where they are standing today. Those who have read the book as a narrative of the battle can now visualize the fighting through the medium of pictures as well as words.

This new introduction also gives me the opportunity to update information about Gettysburg National Military Park with the changes that have been made since the first edition in 2003. The Park Service has continued its replanting of orchards on the battlefield, including the full extent of the famous Peach Orchard. The building of fences to replicate where fences were located in 1863 has also continued, and the removal of non-historic woods and modern buildings from the battlefield has also continued, so that the landscape is now closer to its 1863 appearance than it has been for many decades. The old Visitor Center and Cyclorama building are gone, replaced by a new Visitor Center and Cyclorama venue that opened in 2008. There, fiber-optic maps of each day of the battle have replaced the old electric map. There is no longer an interpretive marker at Barlow's Knoll telling the apocryphal story of a Barlow-Gordon meeting after the war.

The narrative that follows has stood up well over the past twelve years. With the added dimensions of illustrations and many first-hand accounts by participants, this new edition of *Hallowed Ground* will enable a new generation of readers to visualize one of the most important events in American history with greater clarity and understanding than ever before.

—JAMES M. MCPHERSON

PROLOGUE

IN HIS address at the dedication of the cemetery for Union soldiers killed in the battle of Gettysburg, President Abraham Lincoln acknowledged that "in a larger sense, we can not dedicate—we can not consecrate—we can not hallow this ground. The brave men, living and dead, who struggled here, have consecrated it, far above our power to add or detract."

More than any other place in the United States, this battlefield is indeed hallowed ground. Perhaps no word in the American language has greater historical resonance than Gettysburg. For some people Lexington and Concord, or Bunker Hill, or Yorktown, or Omaha Beach would be close rivals. But more Americans visit Gettysburg each year than any of these other battlefields—perhaps than all of them combined.

And Gettysburg resonates far beyond these shores. At least sixty thousand foreigners are among the nearly two million annual visitors to the battlefield. In 1851 the British historian Sir Edward Creasy wrote a famous book titled *Fifteen Decisive Battles of the World*. The last of the fifteen was Waterloo, fought in 1815. After the American Civil War, Creasy published a new edition with a sixteenth decisive battle—Gettysburg.

Gettysburg's Soldiers' National Cemetery is the burial site of the Union dead and is centered on the Federal battle line. Its elegant layout and concentric rings were designed by landscape architect William Saunders, and President Abraham Lincoln dedicated it on November 19, 1863, with his lionized Gettysburg Address.

A contemporary view of the National Cemetery.

During the bicentennial commemorations of the American Revolution in 1976, a delegation of historians from the Soviet Union visited the United States as a goodwill gesture, to take part in these events. A colleague of mine on the history faculty at Princeton University was one of their hosts. When they arrived, he asked them which historic sites they wanted to visit first—perhaps Independence Hall in Philadelphia, or maybe Williamsburg and Yorktown in Virginia, or Lexington and Concord in Massachusetts. But their answer was none of these. They wanted to go first to Gettysburg.

The National Cemetery, ca. 1913.

Why Gettysburg? asked my astonished colleague. It had nothing to do with the American Revolution. To the contrary, replied the Russians; it had everything to do with the Revolution. In Lincoln's words, it ensured that the nation founded in 1776 would not "perish from the earth." These Soviet historians may have been more familiar with Lincoln's Gettysburg Address than was my colleague. They knew that the famous opening words of that address—"Four score and seven years ago"—referred to the founding of the United States in 1776, and

A Gettysburg Electric Railway Company trolley at the entrance to the National Cemetery.

that Gettysburg was the battlefield on which thousands gave the last full measure of devotion that the nation might live. These Russians also wanted to see Gettysburg first because they compared it to their battle of Stalingrad in World War II—it was the costliest battle in America's own Great Patriotic War that turned the tide toward ultimate victory.

In 1896 the United States Supreme Court handed down a decision that has stood for more than a century as a landmark in the struggle for historic preservation of hallowed ground. Not surprisingly, that decision grew out of events surrounding the recent creation of Gettysburg National Military Park. The Gettysburg Electric Railway Company had built a trolley line over the southern part of the battlefield to carry tourists to Devil's Den and the Round Tops. The park wanted to buy the land and restore it to its 1863 appearance, which of course would mean removal of the trolley line. The company refused to sell. The government began proceedings to seize the land under the power of eminent domain. The case went to the Supreme Court, where the government argued that "the ground whereon great conflicts have taken

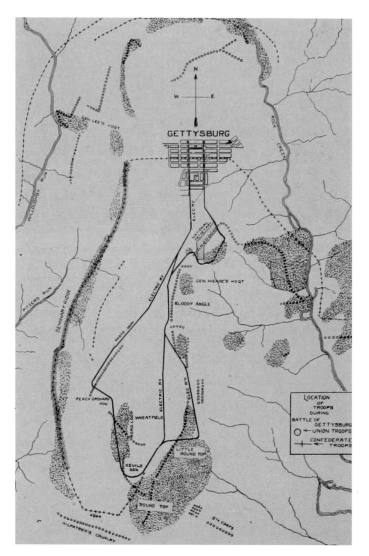

A map of the trolley's route.

place, especially those where great interests or principles were at stake, becomes at once of so much public interest that its preservation is essentially a matter of public concern." Nowhere were such great principles at stake more than at Gettysburg, which embodied "the national idea and the principle of the indissolubility of the Union."

The Court agreed. The justices ruled unanimously that Gettysburg was vested with such importance for the fate of the United States that the government had the right to "take possession of the field of battle, in the name and for the benefit of all the citizens of the country. . . . Such a use seems . . . so closely connected with the welfare of the republic itself as to be within the powers granted Congress by the Constitution for the purpose of protecting and preserving the whole country."

The battle of Gettysburg was an event without equal in its connection "with the welfare of the republic itself," as the Court put it. But what is Gettysburg as a place? It is a battlefield of about ten square miles (five miles from north to south and two miles from east to west, not counting East Cavalry Field) surrounding a county-seat town of about eight thousand people today, 2,400 at the time of the battle in 1863. It is located seventy-five miles north of Washington, 115 miles west of Philadelphia, and only eight miles north of the Mason-Dixon Line, which forms the border between Pennsylvania and Maryland. From the town of Gettysburg a dozen historic (and modern) roads radiate to every point of the compass—a major reason why a great battle was fought there, for the road network enabled the armies to concentrate there quickly after the opening clashes.

Although it is the home of Gettysburg College and of a Lutheran theological seminary, the main business of Gettysburg today is tourism. Most of those nearly two million visitors to the battlefield spend money in town. Many tourist services flourish, from restaurants and motels to shops selling every kind of trinket and relic, from "ghost tours" and a wax museum to bookstores and picture galleries. Some of these businesses are cheek by jowl with the National Military Park, which includes more than four thousand acres on which most of the fighting took place during those first three days of July 1863.

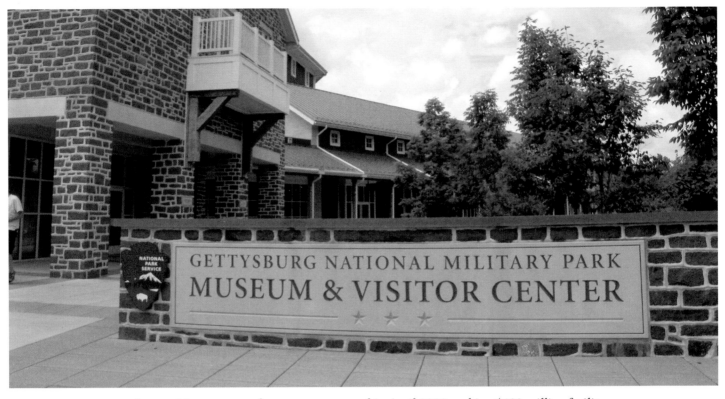

A new visitor center and museum was opened in April 2008 and is a $103 million facility.

No tourists came to Gettysburg before that time. It was then a market town for a large and prosperous agricultural hinterland. The area was a famous fruit-growing region; no fewer than thirty-eight orchards existed on what became the battlefield. All of them are gone today except part of the famous Peach Orchard where the Confederates broke Dan Sickles's line on July 2, plus two ornamental fruit orchards on Cemetery Hill and at the site of the Bliss farm, across which some of the Pickett-Pettigrew attackers marched on July 3. The Park Service has long-term plans to plant replica orchards where they existed in 1863—but don't hold your breath waiting for it to happen.

I have lost count of the number of times I have been to Gettysburg. I have toured the battlefield by car, by bus, on a bicycle, and on foot. Over the past twenty years I have taken Princeton students, alumni, friends, and miscellaneous groups on at least two dozen tours of the battlefield. I have made so many visits to the college and town, as well as the battlefield, that Gettysburg has become almost a second home. I honestly believe that if I were blindfolded and winched down from a helicopter to any spot on the battlefield on a moonlit night, I could remove the blindfold and identify my surroundings within minutes.

I would not have known where I was on many parts of the battlefield in 1863, however. Not only did all those orchards exist then, but there are also some six hundred acres of woods today that were cleared then, and about 150 acres of cleared land today that were wooded in 1863. Another six hundred acres of woods that existed in the same places then as now were woodlots in 1863, where farmers harvested dead trees and some live ones for fuel and fencing.

They also allowed livestock to graze in some of these woodlots, which kept them free from undergrowth. Many of the woodlots were therefore open and parklike in 1863, enabling troops to move through and fight in them where saplings and undergrowth today would make such activities impossible.

The Park Service plans to remove 150 acres of woods that did not exist in 1863, to reforest fifty acres (plus the orchards) where woods did exist in 1863, and to cull some trees from the six hundred acres of woodlots. When they have done so, it will be easier to see and understand the lines of sight, approach, and combat that existed in 1863 (though the culled woodlots will soon grow up in brush and saplings again in the absence of grazing livestock, for which the Park Service has no plans). Until (and even after) this cutting and culling happens, however, the first thing a tour guide must tell listeners is to imagine a cleared field or a parklike woodlot where there are thick woods today, or imagine an orchard or a grove where there are none today. Such a feat of imagination is not always easy.

What brought those 165,000 soldiers—75,000 Confederate, 90,000 Union—to Gettysburg during the first three days of July 1863? Why did they lock themselves in such a deathgrip across these once bucolic fields until 11,000 of them were killed and mortally wounded, another 29,000 were wounded and survived, and about 10,000 were "missing"—mostly captured. By way of comparison, those 50,000 casualties at Gettysburg—27,000 Confederate,* 23,000 Union—were almost ten times the number of American casualties on D-Day, June 6, 1944. What was accomplished by all of this carnage? Join me for a walk on this hallowed ground, where we will try to answer these questions.

---

* Because of incomplete records, the number of Confederate casualties at Gettysburg is an estimate. Such estimates range from 23,000 to 28,000.

Each year millions of people visit Gettysburg sites, such as these tourists climbing Devil's Den.

DAY ONE

July 1, 1863

WE'LL BEGIN our tour three miles northwest of the Gettysburg town square, at the intersection of Knoxlyn Road and US Route 30, the historic Chambersburg Pike. Here, on the morning of July 1, were posted the outlying pickets of the Eighth Illinois Cavalry. As the sun burned away the mist, they spotted a column of Confederate infantry marching toward them. At 7:30 AM, Lieutenant Marcellus Jones rested a breechloading Sharps carbine on a fence rail and fired at the enemy. It was the first shot in the largest battle ever fought in the western hemisphere. Why were these soldiers here, more than one hundred miles north of the Rappahannock River in Virginia, where they had confronted each other until only three weeks earlier? After scrambling up the steep bank on the north side of Route 30 to look at the small "first shot" marker to the left of an abandoned house, let's head southeast on Route 30 almost two miles to the parking lot behind the guide station at the National Park entrance. From there we'll walk a hundred yards south to get away from the traffic noise. Here is a good place to answer the question: What brought these two armies to Gettysburg?

A chromolithograph made after the painting Battle of Gettysburg *by French artist Paul Philippoteaux.*

A view of the northern portion of the battlefield, shown from west of the town near the seminary.

Those who have watched the electric map presentation at the National Park Visitor Center have learned the apparently paradoxical fact that the Confederates approached Gettysburg from the north and the Union army came up from the south. Having seized the initiative and invaded Pennsylvania, Southern troops got there first while the Army of the Potomac followed cautiously, remaining between the invaders and Washington to the southeast. Thus, when fate brought the armies together at Gettysburg, Union soldiers arrived from the south and southeast and Confederates from the northwest and north.

The preceding six months had been a low point for the Union cause. On December 13, 1862, the Army of the Potomac, commanded by Major General Ambrose E. Burnside, had attacked General Robert E. Lee's Army of Northern Virginia at Fredericksburg on the Rappahannock. There the Yankees had sustained a disastrous and humiliating defeat.

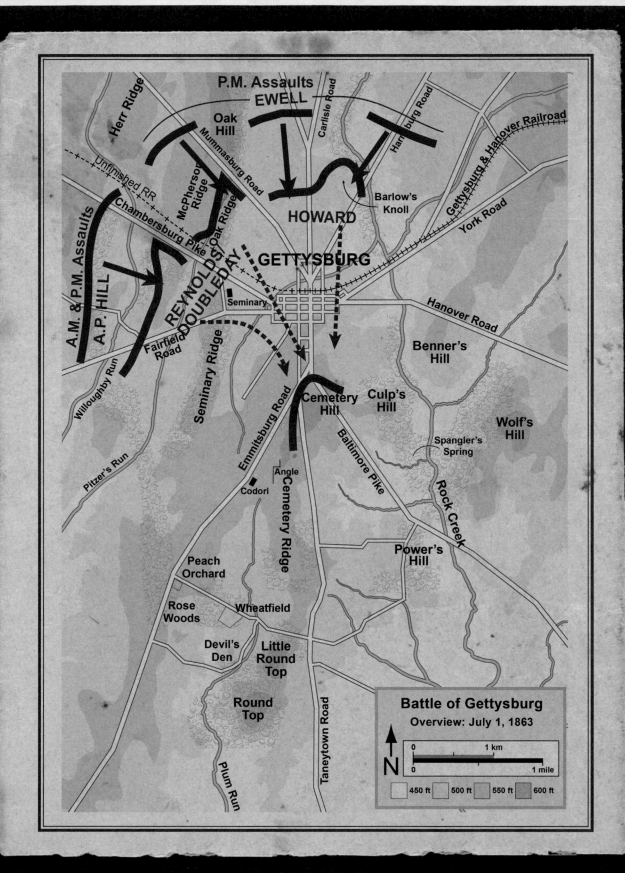

A map of the first day of battle.

HARPER'S WEEKLY.

A JOURNAL OF CIVILIZATION.

VOL. VI.—No. 313.] NEW YORK, SATURDAY, DECEMBER 27, 1862. [SINGLE COPIES SIX CENTS.
[$2.50 PER YEAR IN ADVANCE.

Entered according to Act of Congress, in the Year 1862, by Harper & Brothers, in the Clerk's Office of the District Court for the Southern District of New York.

THE ATTACK ON FREDERICKSBURG—THE FORLORN HOPE SCALING THE HILL.—[See Page 830.]

The forlorn cover of a Harper's Weekly *issue in which it was printed of the North, "The people have borne, silently and grimly, imbecility, treachery, failure, privation, loss of friends."*

Northern spirits plummeted. "The people have borne, silently and grimly, imbecility, treachery, failure, privation, loss of friends," editorialized the leading Northern magazine, *Harper's Weekly*, "but they cannot be expected to suffer that such massacres as this at Fredericksburg shall be repeated." When Lincoln heard the news of Fredericksburg, he said, "If there is a worse place than Hell, I am in it."

Morale in the Army of the Potomac sank to its lowest point during the winter of 1862–63. "The army is tired with its hard and terrible experience," wrote twenty-one-year-old Captain Oliver Wendell Holmes Jr., who was recovering from the second of three wounds he would receive in the war (the third would keep him out of the battle of Gettysburg). "I've pretty much made up my mind that the South have achieved their independence."

Things would get worse for the North before they got better. At the end of April, a new commander of the Army of the Potomac, Major General Joseph Hooker, launched an offensive

Major General Ambrose E. Burnside, 1824–1881.

Union Major General Joseph Hooker yielded to Lee at Chancellorsville.

at the crossroads hostelry of Chancellorsville, a few miles west of Fredericksburg. After getting in the enemy's rear and gaining a tactical advantage, however, Hooker lost his nerve and yielded the initiative to Lee. The ensuing battle of Chancellorsville, May 1–5, 1863, marked Lee's most brilliant achievement. Facing greatly superior numbers, he divided his army three times in a series of flank and frontal attacks that bewildered Hooker. Although Lee's ablest subordinate, Lieutenant General Stonewall Jackson, was wounded by friendly fire on May 2, the Army of Northern Virginia went on to inflict another humiliating defeat on the enemy.

Jackson's death from pneumonia (which set in after his wounding) on May 10 tempered the joy in the South produced by Chancellorsville. Nevertheless, confidence abounded that

Confederate General Robert E. Lee.

one more Confederate victory in this theater would offset Union successes in Mississippi and win Confederate independence. Lee decided to carry the war into Pennsylvania in a bid to conquer a peace on Northern soil. To the Confederate government in Richmond, Lee presented the dazzling prospect that an invasion of Pennsylvania would remove the enemy threat on the Rappahannock, take the armies out of war-ravaged Virginia and enable the Confederates to supply themselves from the rich Pennsylvania countryside, and relieve the pressure on Confederate armies in the west by compelling Union forces there to send reinforcements to the east. Lee's plan might also strengthen Northern Peace Democrats (so-called Copperheads) in their arguments for an armistice and peace negotiations; discredit Lincoln and

The Union defeat at the Battle of Fredericksburg sunk morale in the North as it raised the spirits of the South.

Confederate President Jefferson Davis.

his war policies, including the Emancipation Proclamation issued five months earlier; encourage European diplomatic recognition of the Confederacy; and perhaps even capture Harrisburg or Baltimore and hold the city hostage for a cease-fire and negotiations.

Confederate President Jefferson Davis told Lee to go ahead. In the post-Chancellorsville aura of invincibility, anything seemed possible for the Army of Northern Virginia. "There never were such men in an army before," wrote Lee in June 1863 as his troops started north. "They will go anywhere and do anything if properly led." After Jackson's death, Lee had reorganized the army from two corps (under Jackson and Lieutenant General James Longstreet) into three corps of three divisions each, commanded by Longstreet, A. P. Hill, and Richard Ewell (who got most of Jackson's old corps). Both Hill and Ewell earned their promotion to corps command with the rank of lieutenant general by their records as successful division commanders under Jackson—though Ewell had only recently returned to the army after losing a leg at Second Manassas the previous August. Major General Jeb Stuart commanded the army's cavalry corps. All of these men except Longstreet were Virginians, as were five of the nine division commanders—a source of complaint and jealousy among some non-Virginians in an army two-thirds of whose soldiers were from states other than Virginia.

There never were such men in an army before. They will go anywhere and do anything if properly led.

During the second week of June, the Army of Northern Virginia moved north through the Shenandoah Valley toward the Potomac River, keeping the Blue Ridge Mountains between themselves and Union cavalry that probed the mountain gaps to track the enemy. The Northern cavalry gave a good account of itself for almost the first time in this theater, especially at the battle of Brandy Station (near Culpeper, Virginia) on June 9. Some of the best fighting in these cavalry actions was done by a Union division under Brigadier General John Buford, a native of Kentucky whose cousin was a brigadier general in the Confederate army.

*The Confederate commanders at Gettysburg included (clockwise from top left)
Lieutenant Generals Longstreet, Ewell, and Hill and Major General Stuart.*

LEE'S SUPPLY TRAIN

By Abner Doubleday

Lee was startled to learn from a countryman who came in on the 28th [of June] that Hooker was at Frederick, and not south of the Potomac, as he had supposed. He saw at once that his communications with Richmond, about which he was so solicitous, were greatly endangered, for the Union army could be formed to interpose between him and Williamsport, and still keep a safe line of retreat open to Washington. This might not be so great a misfortune to the enemy as regards food and forage; for he

A rebel pontoon with its supply train moving along the Potomac.

could probably live on the country for some time, by making predatory excursions in different directions, but when it came to obtaining fresh supplies of ammunition, the matter would become very serious. An army only carries a limited amount of this into the field and must rely upon frequent convoys to keep up the supply, which is constantly decreasing from the partial engagements and skirmishes, so prevalent in a hostile country.

The wisdom of Hooker's policy in desiring to assail the rebel communications is demonstrated by the fact that Lee immediately turned back. The head of the serpent faced about as soon as its tail was trodden upon. He came to the conclusion to prevent an attack against his rear by threatening Baltimore with his whole force. This would necessarily cause the Union army to march further east to confront him, and thus prevent it from operating in heavy force in the Cumberland Valley. Accordingly on the night of the 28th, Lee sent expresses to all his corps commanders to concentrate at Gettysburg. If he had known that Meade was about to withdraw all the troops acting against his line of retreat he would probably have gone on and taken Harrisburg.

Jeb Stuart's Confederate horsemen had been surprised and roughly handled at Brandy Station. Stuart's ego may have been bruised by the criticism this affair provoked in the South. His daring exploits and accurate scouting reports during the previous year had won Stuart deserved fame. He dressed the part of a dashing cavalier: knee-high boots, elbow-length gauntlets, a red-lined cape with a yellow sash, and a felt hat with pinned-up brim and ostrich-feather plume. After Brandy Station, he was determined to dispel criticism and live up to his reputation by performing some new bold and dramatic deed.

Two weeks later an opportunity arose. After screening the Confederate infantry's advance northward by defending the Blue Ridge passes from probing Union horsemen, Stuart got permission from Lee to move into Pennsylvania east of the Blue Ridge–South Mountain range, provided he always remained in contact with the infantry through couriers and was capable of rejoining the main body at any time. This Stuart failed to do. Taking his three best brigades, he allowed the northward-slogging Union army to separate him from the Army of Northern Virginia for a full week, depriving Lee of his cavalry "eyes" at a crucial time. That is why the first contact on July 1 at the site of the "first shot" marker occurred between Union *cavalry* and Confederate *infantry* advancing without the usual cavalry screen and scouts to determine the enemy's position and strength.

Nevertheless, the hot days of late June seemed to signify the pinnacle of Confederate success. Ewell's corps, in advance, had bowled over and captured most of a four-thousand-man Union force blocking their way at Winchester, Virginia, and had crossed the Potomac into Maryland and Pennsylvania. One of Ewell's divisions penetrated to the Susquehanna River at Wrightsville, while two others occupied Carlisle and threatened Harrisburg and the Pennsylvania Railroad bridge over the Susquehanna, the destruction of which was one of Lee's goals in the campaign. This initial success seemed to mark Ewell as a worthy successor to Jackson. He even rivaled the famously eccentric Jackson in eccentricity, with an ulcer-induced diet of hulled wheat in milk and an egg yolk. He had a beaked nose and a habit of cocking his

A cavalry charge at the Battle of Brandy Station.

The "first shot" marker sits on what is now the side of Route 30.

head to one side, which reminded observers of a bird. Ewell had recently married a widow, whom he absentmindedly referred to as "Mrs. Brown."

While Ewell's divisions were threatening Harrisburg and Wrightsville on June 28, Lee, with the rest of the army, was at Chambersburg, twenty-five miles northwest of Gettysburg. The campaign seemed a smashing success so far. The invaders stripped the countryside and towns of all the cattle, horses, shoes, and food they could find. Pennsylvanians were in a panic. Contrary to time-honored legend, Lee's orders against pillage of civilian property were honored in the breach by many soldiers. "The wrath of southern vengeance will be wreaked upon the pennsilvanians & all property belonging to the abolition horde which we cross," wrote a Virginian. A North Carolina soldier confessed in a letter home that "our men did very bad in MD. and Penn. They robed every house . . . not only of eatables but of everything they could lay their hands on. They tore up dresses to bits and broke all the furniture."

All that remained was to find the Army of the Potomac and whip it. Despite the troubling absence of Stuart, which left him without accurate intelligence about the enemy's whereabouts, Lee exuded confidence. According to one of his subordinates, Lee said that when he located the Army of the Potomac, "I shall throw an overwhelming force on their advance, crush it, follow up the success, drive one corps back on another, and by successive repulses and surprises create a panic and virtually destroy the army. [Then] the war will be over and we shall achieve the recognition of our independence."

This turned out to be the pride that goeth before a fall. The Army of the Potomac was coming, with more speed and élan than Lee realized. That army had a new commander. When the Confederates entered Pennsylvania, Lincoln saw an opportunity as well as a threat, an opportunity to cut off and cripple the enemy far from his home base. The president told Secretary of the Navy Gideon Welles that "we cannot help beating them, if we have the man." But Lincoln became convinced that Hooker was not the man. The general had begun to fret that the enemy outnumbered him, that he needed reinforcements, that the government was not supporting him. To Lincoln these complaints sounded as though Hooker was looking for an excuse not to fight. When the general submitted his resignation over a dispute about the Union garrison at Harpers Ferry, Lincoln accepted it on June 28 and promoted a surprised Major General George Gordon Meade to command.

The destruction in Fredericksburg after the battle.

MEADE ASSUMES COMMAND AND GOES TO GETTYSBURG

MEADE'S OFFICIAL REPORTS

From: Frederick, Maryland, 7 AM, June 28, 1863.
To: H. W. Halleck, General-in-Chief:

The order placing me in command of this army is received. As a soldier I obey it, and to the utmost of my ability will execute it. Totally unexpected as it has been, and in ignorance of the exact condition of the troops and position of the enemy, I can only now say that it appears to me I must move towards the Susquehanna, keeping Washington and Baltimore well covered, and if the enemy is checked in his attempt to cross the Susquehanna, or if he turns towards Baltimore, to give him battle. I would say that I trust that every available man that can be spared will be sent to me, as, from all accounts, the enemy is in strong force. So soon as I can post myself up I will communicate more in detail.

◇◇◇◇◇◇◇◇◇◇◇◇

From: Frederick, Maryland, June 29, 1863.
To: General Halleck

If Lee is moving for Baltimore, I expect to get between his main army and that place. If he is crossing the Susquehanna, I shall rely upon General Couch, with his force, holding him until I can fall upon his rear and give him battle. . . . I shall incline to the right towards the Baltimore and Harrisburg Road, to cover that and draw supplies from there if circumstances will permit it; my main objective point being, of course, Lee's army, which I am satisfied has all passed through Hagerstown towards Chambersburg. My endeavors will be in my movements to hold my force well together, with the hope of falling on some portion of Lee's army in detail . . .

My main point being to find and fight the enemy, I shall have to submit to the cavalry raids around me, in some measure; and also, in

Major General George Gordon Meade.

speaking of the impossibility, in the absence of telegraphic communication, of his giving orders to General Schenck, in Baltimore, or to the troops on the Potomac, in his rear, or to General Couch, at Harrisburg, he said: These circumstances are beyond my control.

◇◇◇◇◇◇◇◇◇◇◇◇◇◇◇

MEADE'S LETTERS TO HIS WIFE

JUST BEFORE LEAVING FREDERICK CITY SEIZED THE FIRST OPPORTUNITY THAT HAD OFFERED TO WRITE PERSONALLY TO MRS. MEADE AS TO THE WONDROUS CHANGE IN HIS AFFAIRS.

FROM: Headquarters, Army of the Potomac, Frederick City, Maryland, June 29, 1863.
TO: Mrs. George G. Meade

It has pleased Almighty God to place me in the trying position that for some time past we have been talking about. Yesterday morning, at 3 AM, I was aroused from my sleep by an officer from Washington entering my tent, and after waking me up, saying he had come to give me trouble. At first I thought that it was either to relieve or arrest me, and promptly replied to him, that my conscience was clear, void of offense towards any man; I was prepared for his bad news. He then handed me a communication to read; which I found was an order relieving Hooker from the command and assigning me to it. As, dearest, you know how reluctant we both have been to see me placed in this position, and as it appears to be God's will for some good purpose—at any rate, as a soldier, I had nothing to do but accept and exert my utmost abilities to command success. This, so help me God, I will do, and trusting to Him, who in his good pleasure has thought it proper to place me where I am, I shall pray for strength and power to get through with the task assigned me. I cannot write you all I would like. I am moving at once against Lee, whom I am in hopes Couch will at least check for a few days; if so, a battle will decide the fate of our country and our cause. Pray earnestly, pray for the success of my country, (for it is my success besides). Love to all. I will try and write often, but must depend on George.

AFTER MOVING THROUGHOUT THE DAY, IN THE EVENING HE WROTE AGAIN:

From: Headquarters, Army of the Potomac, Middleburg, Maryland, June 29, 1863.
To: Mrs. George G. Meade

We are marching as fast as we can to relieve Harrisburg, but have to keep a sharp lookout that the rebels don't turn around us and get at Washington and Baltimore in our rear. They have a cavalry force in our rear, destroying railroads, etc., with the view of getting me to turn back; but I shall not do it. I am going straight at them, and will settle this thing one way or the other. The men are in good spirits; we have been reinforced so as to have equal numbers with the enemy, and with God's blessing I hope to be successful. Good-by!

★ ★ ★

This map of the full Gettysburg campaign shows the movements of the North and South leading up to the battle.

The Army of the Potomac on the move.

Meade was the fourth commander of the Army of the Potomac. He had compiled a solid if not brilliant record as a division commander, and he had not taken part in the cliquish internecine rivalries that had plagued the officer corps of that army. Meade's testy temper and large, piercing eyes crowned by a high forehead caused one soldier to describe him as "a God-damned old goggle-eyed snapping turtle." But Meade's tactical skills, including the effective use of terrain and reserves, would play a large part in the coming battle.

As the Army of the Potomac moved north to confront the invaders, its morale rose with the latitude. Civilians in western Maryland and southern Pennsylvania cheered them, in contrast to the hostile curses they were accustomed to hearing in Virginia. "Our men are three times as enthusiastic as they have been in Virginia," wrote a Union surgeon. "The idea that Pennsylvania is invaded and that we are fighting on our own soil, proper, influences them strongly. They are more determined than I have ever before seen them."

These soldiers had been toughened to a flinty self-reliance in earlier campaigns under bumbling leaders. They "have something of the English bull-dog in them," wrote a Massachusetts officer. "You can whip them time and again, but the next fight they go into, they are as full of pluck as ever. . . . Some day or other we shall have our turn."

Lead musket balls and Minié balls were common ammunition.

That day was coming soon. On the night of June 28, a civilian spy employed by General Longstreet brought word to Lee and Longstreet in Chambersburg that the Army of the Potomac was concentrated just south of the Pennsylvania border and was moving north. Chagrined that he had not learned this information from Stuart, Lee was nevertheless convinced that he must act quickly lest the enemy get between his divided forces. He sent couriers to recall Ewell's divisions from Wrightsville and Carlisle. Meanwhile, Major General Henry Heth's division of A. P. Hill's corps marched at dawn toward Gettysburg on the Chambersburg Pike, where at 7:30 they encountered Lieutenant Marcellus Jones and his advance picket post.

. . . the Army of the Potomac was concentrated just south of the Pennsylvania border and was moving north.

This confrontation introduces the first of many supposed "myths" about Gettysburg that continue to provoke arguments to this day. Generations of historians—and battlefield guides—have said that the advance brigade of Heth's division was heading to Gettysburg to find a rumored supply of shoes in town. Young people especially are captivated by the story that the battle of Gettysburg started because of shoes. Recently, however, some historians have debunked this anecdote as a myth. There was no shoe factory or warehouse in Gettysburg, they point out; the twenty-two shoemakers listed in the 1860 census as living in Gettysburg were barely sufficient to make or repair the footwear worn by county residents. And if there had been a surplus of shoes in town, they would have been cleaned out by Brigadier General

John Gordon's brigade of Major General Jubal Early's division when they came through Gettysburg five days earlier.

The shoe story, claim these historians, was concocted by General Heth (pronounced Heath) to explain why he blundered into a firefight contrary to Lee's orders not to bring on a battle until the army was concentrated. Heth said that he thought the Union pickets he encountered on the Chambersburg Pike were merely local militia who could be brushed aside, so he kept going to "get those shoes."

The revisionists have made one good point: there were no shoes in Gettysburg except those worn by the inhabitants still in town (many had fled). But that does not necessarily discredit the shoe story. The Confederates may well have thought there were shoes; several of them later said so. In any case, the anecdote serves an important purpose because it illustrates that the battle of Gettysburg began as a "meeting engagement," or "encounter engagement." Neither commander intended to fight at Gettysburg; the battle built up step by step from that first encounter on the Chambersburg Pike. Let us concede that the shoe story can neither be proved nor disproved; let us follow the current fashion and call Heth's advance a "reconnaissance in force" to probe toward the enemy; the end result was the same.

Though the shoe story may be a myth, the fact that soldiers were in need of shoes throughout the war is not.

For these were no militia that Heth's infantry ran into; they were troopers from John Buford's cavalry division who had fought so well at Brandy Station three weeks earlier. Scouting ahead of the rest of the Union army, two of Buford's brigades (about 2,700 men) had entered Gettysburg the day before and discovered signs of the enemy on the road several miles to the northwest. Buford sized up the terrain of ridges and hills around Gettysburg, and the road network that would facilitate concentration of the army there. He sent word south to Major General John Reynolds, commander of the nearest Union infantry (First Corps) near Emmitsburg, Maryland, that he intended to hold those ridges as long as he could against the enemy force he sensed was coming. He asked Reynolds to get his infantry there as soon as possible in the morning. Thus it was Buford who made the crucial decision that led to the battle being fought at Gettysburg. For that distinction he earned one of the statues on the battlefield, portraying Buford on foot with binoculars in hand looking toward the northwest. There are seven equestrian statues at Gettysburg, all of infantry commanders (including army commanders Lee and Meade); the most prominent Union cavalry commander is memorialized in bronze on foot. Go figure.

The bronze Buford stands on McPherson Ridge (named after a local man whose farm was located there—no relation to me) a mile and three-quarters back toward Gettysburg from where Lieutenant Jones fired the first shot. Jones sent back word of his encounter, and then skirmished with the enemy in a fighting withdrawal to Buford's first line on Herr Ridge. This line held for a time as Heth, recognizing that he was not confronting militia, deployed two brigades to run over these pesky Yankee horsemen. Before this could happen, those horsemen pulled back across Willoughby Run to McPherson Ridge, where Buford had established his main line, with one brigade south of the Pike and the other north of it. Let's walk east across a swale south of the white barn (the only structure of the McPherson farm that survives) to the slight ridgeline marked by several monuments and cannons along Reynolds Avenue. This was the final line held by Buford's cavalry.

The memorial statue of Major General John Buford.

BUFORD MAKES CONTACT WITH THE CONFEDERATES

BUFORD'S OFFICIAL REPORT

FROM: Gettysburg, July 1, 10:10 AM
TO: General Meade

The enemy's force (A. P. Hill's) are advancing on me at this point and driving my pickets and skirmishers very rapidly. There is also a large force at Heidlersburg, that is driving my pickets at that point from that direction. General Reynolds is advancing, and is within three miles of this point, with his leading division. I am positive that the whole of A. P. Hill's force is advancing.

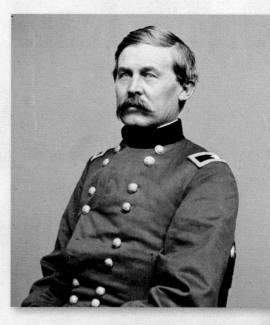

Major General John Buford.

★ ★ ★

The Lutheran seminary building as it stands today.

Heth's division numbered seven thousand men, but he deployed only half of them. Most of Buford's cavalry fought dismounted, a tactic increasingly prevalent during the Civil War, when the greater range and accuracy of the new rifled muskets over the old smoothbores made mounted charges against infantry suicidally obsolete. One of every four troopers held four horses about two hundred yards to the rear while his comrades fought. Although outnumbered, Buford's men had one advantage. Like most Union horse soldiers, they were armed by this stage of the war with Sharps single-shot breechloading carbines. Infantrymen carried single-shot muzzle-loading rifled muskets. These weapons had a longer range and greater hitting power than cavalry carbines, but even a good infantryman could get off only two or three shots a minute while a trooper armed with a breechloader could fire twice as fast.

As Heth built up more and more power, Buford climbed to the cupola of the Lutheran seminary building (still there) on the next ridgeline, appropriately named Seminary Ridge. He looked anxiously to the south for Reynolds and his promised reinforcements. As Buford's tired troopers were about to give way, Reynolds came galloping across the fields, followed at double time by two brigades of his leading division. One of them was the famous Iron Brigade, containing one Indiana, one Michigan, and three Wisconsin regiments, and considered the toughest unit in the army. As Reynolds personally led this brigade into line at about 10:30 AM, he suddenly slumped in the saddle and fell from his horse with a bullet through the base of his skull—the first and highest-ranking general killed at Gettysburg. A small monument on the east side of the Herbst Woods (now usually called McPherson's Woods or sometimes Reynolds' Woods) marks the spot where Reynolds fell.

MEADE'S ORDERS TO REYNOLDS

OFFICIAL ORDERS

The telegraphic intelligence received from General Couch, with the various movements reported by Buford, seem to indicate the concentration of the enemy either at Chambersburg, or at a point situated somewhere on a line drawn between Chambersburg and York, through Heidlersburg, and to the north of Gettysburg.

The Commanding General cannot decide whether it is his best policy to move to attack until he learns something more definite of the point at which the enemy is concentrating. This he hopes to do during the day. Meanwhile, he would like to have your views upon the subject, at least so far as concerns your position.

If the enemy is concentrated to the right of Gettysburg, that point would not, at first glance, seem to be a proper strategic point of concentration for this army. If the enemy is concentrating in front of Gettysburg, or to the left of it, the General is not sufficiently informed of the nature of the country to judge of its character either for an offensive or defensive position. The number of the enemy are estimated at about 92,000 infantry, with 270 pieces of artillery, and his cavalry, from six to eight thousand. Our numbers ought to equal it, and with the arrival of General French's command, which should get up to-morrow, exceed it, if not too much weakened by straggling and fatigue.

The General having assumed command in obedience to orders, with the position of affairs leaving no time to learn the condition of the army as to morale and proportionate strength, compared with its last return, would gladly receive from you any suggestions as to the points laid down in this note. He feels that you know more of the condition of the troops in your vicinity, and the country, than he does.

Major General John F. Reynolds.

General Humphreys, who is at Emmettsburg with the Third Corps, the General considers an excellent adviser as to the nature of the country for defensive or offensive operations. If near enough to call him to consultation with you, please do so, without interference with the responsibilities that devolve upon you both. You have all the information which the General has received, and the General would like to have your views.

The movement of your Corps to Gettysburg was ordered before the positive knowledge of the enemy's withdrawal from Harrisburg and concentration was received.

★ ★ ★

Major General John Reynolds's fall at Gettysburg.

*A Sharps breechloading carbine
commonly used by Union cavalry.*

A quarter-mile to the north, across the road and next to Buford's monument, is a large equestrian statue of Reynolds. It introduces us to another dispute about a supposed Gettysburg myth. Two of the hooves of Reynolds's horse are raised. Generations of battlefield guides have explained that this pose conforms to a pattern indicating that the rider was killed in the battle. If one hoof is off the ground, the rider was wounded—and that is true of the equestrian monument to Major General Winfield Scott Hancock, who was wounded at Gettysburg. If all four of the horse's feet are on the ground, the rider was unharmed in the battle—and that also is true of all the rest of Gettysburg's monuments (save the newest one—of which more later). Some park personnel and guides, however, now debunk this "myth" as well, and insist that the relationship between hooves and the rider's fate is purely coincidental. But that strikes me as unlikely. For centuries a convention has existed among sculptors of equestrian statues to symbolize the rider's fate in battle by the placement of the horse's hooves. So I will continue to tell that story about the equestrian monuments at Gettysburg.

*Left: Reynolds's equestrian monument. Right: Major General Abner
Doubleday's monument on Doubleday Avenue at Gettysburg.*

Confederate prisoners captured at Gettysburg.

After Reynolds's death, Major General Abner Doubleday took command of the Union First Corps. (Doubleday did not invent baseball—that indeed is a myth.) The Iron Brigade counterattacked one of Heth's brigades through the Herbst Woods and down the slope to Willoughby Run. These woods were open and parklike at the time, even more than they are today after the Park Service's effort to cull the woods to something resembling their 1863 character. The yelling bluecoats smashed into the right flank of Brigadier General James M. Archer's brigade of Tennesseans and Alabamians, capturing many of the men plus Archer himself, the first of Lee's generals to suffer this ignominy. Grinning, a big Union private named Patrick Maloney escorted a scowling Archer to the rear. Behind the lines they ran into General Doubleday, who had known Archer well in the prewar army. "Archer! I'm glad to see you," said Doubleday as he strode forward to shake hands. "Well, I'm not glad to see you by a damn sight," growled Archer as he turned away.

THE DEATH
OF REYNOLDS

OFFICIAL REPORTS, GENERAL HOWARD
TO GENERAL MEADE

Headquarters Eleventh Corps, July 1, 5 PM

First. Gen. Reynolds attacked the enemy as soon as he arrived, with one division, about 10:45 o'clock, AM. He moved to the front of the town, driving in the enemy's advance for about half a mile, when he met with a strong force of A. P. Hill's corps. I pushed up as fast as I could by a parallel road; placed my corps in position on his right. General Reynolds was killed at eleven and a quarter AM. I assumed command of the two corps and sent word to Slocum and Sickles to move up. I have fought the enemy from that time to this. The First Corps fell back, when outflanked on its left, to a stronger position, when the Eleventh Corps was ordered back also, to a stronger position. General Hancock arrived at 4 PM, and communicated his intentions. I am still holding on at this time. Slocum is near, but will not come up to assume command.

◇◇◇◇◇◇◇◇◇◇◇

Where Reynolds was killed.

HANCOCK APPOINTED AND ARRIVES AT THE BATTLE

A few minutes before 1 PM, I received orders to proceed in person to the front, and assume command of the First, Third, and Eleventh Corps, in consequence of the death of Major-General Reynolds. Having been fully informed by the major-general commanding as to his intentions, I was instructed by him to give the necessary directions upon my arrival at the front for the movement of troops and trains to the rear toward the line of battle he had selected, should I deem it expedient to do so. If the ground was suitable, and circumstances made it wise, I was directed to establish the line of battle at Gettysburg.

—Gen. Winfield Hancock

★ ★ ★

RECOLLECTIONS ON THE DEATH OF REYNOLDS

By Abner Doubleday

Both parties were now trying to obtain possession of the woods. Archer's rebel brigade, preceded by a skirmish line, was crossing Willoughby's Run to enter them on one side as the Iron Brigade went in on the other. General Reynolds was on horseback in the edge of the woods, surrounded by his staff. He felt some anxiety as to the result, and turned his head frequently to see if our troops would be up in time. While looking back in this way, a rebel sharpshooter shot him through the back of the head, the bullet coming out near the eye. He fell dead in an instant, without a word. The country sustained great loss in his death. I lamented him as almost a life-long companion. We were at West Point together, and had served in the same regiment—the old 3d Artillery—upon first entering service, along with our present Commander-in-Chief, General Sherman, and General George H. Thomas. When quite young we had fought in the same battles in Mexico. There was little time, however, to indulge in these recollections. The situation was very peculiar. The rebel left under Davis had driven in Cutler's brigade and our left under Morrow had charged into the woods, preceded by the 2d Wisconsin under Colonel Fairchild, swept suddenly and unexpectedly around the right flank of Archer's brigade, and captured a large part of it, including Archer himself. The fact is, the enemy were careless and underrated us, thinking, it is said, that they had only militia to contend with. The Iron Brigade had a different head-gear from the rest of the army and were recognized at once by their old antagonists. Some of the latter were heard to exclaim: "There are those d----d black-hatted fellows again! 'Taint no militia. It's the Army of the Potomac."

General Abner Doubleday.

John Burns became known as the Hero of Gettysburg.

Just north of the Iron Brigade fought Colonel Roy Stone's "Bucktail Brigade" of three Pennsylvania regiments, including the 150th. That morning, one of those twenty-two shoe-makers listed in the census, seventy-two-year-old John Burns, left home and headed out to the scene of fighting on McPherson's farm. Incensed by this invasion of his town, he picked up a musket from a wounded soldier of the 150th and fought part of the day with that regiment and later with the Iron Brigade. Burns sustained three wounds and became a local legend in Gettysburg for the remaining nine years of his life. After his death, Burns gained the distinction of being the oldest person to be memorialized by a Civil War monument, which stands on Stone Avenue halfway between the monuments to the 150th Pennsylvania and Seventh Wisconsin.

About the time Archer was captured, other Union regiments trapped and captured a couple hundred Mississippians in the cut of an unfinished railroad bed just north of the Chambersburg Pike. In March 1997 a ranger from Yellowstone National Park was on a bus-man's holiday, touring the Gettysburg battlefield. As he walked along this railroad cut, he noticed bones protruding from the bank where it had been washed away by heavy winter rains. They turned out to be the remains of a soldier who was killed by a massive head wound in the fighting there on July 1. No clothing or anything else that might have identified him as Union or Confederate could be found.

Four months later, in a solemn ceremony on the 134th anniversary of his death, this unknown soldier was interred in the National Cemetery with full military honors. I was privileged to pronounce his eulogy and to receive from the U.S. Marine Corps unit that served as his honor guard the American flag that had covered his casket before burial. The most notable feature of this event was the attendance of two genuine Civil War widows—the last of their kind—women who had been married as teenagers in the 1920s to elderly Civil War veterans. Both were now in their nineties, and watched the ceremonies from their wheelchairs. One was white, from Alabama; the other was black, from Colorado.

Back to July 1, 1863. By early afternoon, Heth's attack had spent itself. Union lines had held firm along the Chambersburg Pike. Meanwhile two divisions of the Eleventh Corps had followed the First Corps onto the field and taken up positions in open fields due north of town to confront two divisions of Ewell's corps reported to be approaching from that direction.

Neither Lee nor Meade was yet at Gettysburg. But, contrary to their intentions, what had started as a skirmish had developed into a full-scale battle. Lee was riding toward Gettysburg that morning. As he approached a gap in the South Mountain range at Cashtown, eight miles northwest of Gettysburg, the alarming sound of artillery reached his ears. Puzzled, and frustrated by the lack of cavalry to keep him informed of what was happening, he spurred forward. "I cannot think what has become of Stuart," he said in irritation. "I am in ignorance of what we have in front of us here. It may be the whole Federal army, it may be only a detachment. If it is the whole Federal force, we must fight a battle here." Lee bid farewell to Longstreet, whose corps brought up the rear, and rode ahead toward the guns of Gettysburg to find out what was going on.

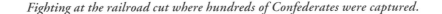

Fighting at the railroad cut where hundreds of Confederates were captured.

GENERAL R. H. ANDERSON MEETS LEE ON THE FIRST DAY IN CASHTOWN

By James Longstreet

About twelve o'clock I received a message notifying me that General Lee desired to see me. I found General Lee intently listening to the fire of the guns, and very much disturbed and depressed. At length he said, more to himself than to me, 'I cannot think what has become of Stuart. I ought to have heard from him long before now. He may have met with disaster, but I hope not. In the absence of reports from him, I am in ignorance as to what we have in front of us here. It may be the whole Federal army, or it may be only a detachment. If it is the whole Federal force, we must fight a battle here. If we do not gain a victory, those defiles and gorges which we passed this morning will shelter us from disaster.

General Robert E. Lee.

*Confederate troops from North Carolina attacking the Federal
line on the first day of the Battle of Gettysburg.*

Lee arrived a little after 2:00 PM to find Heth preparing for a new attack. From a mile to the north came additional sounds of battle. One of Ewell's divisions had arrived and gone into action against the right flank of the Union First Corps, and a second was preparing to attack the Eleventh Corps position. Another of A. P. Hill's divisions, commanded by Major General Dorsey Pender, was ready to go in behind Heth. Lee was still reluctant to commit these divisions until Longstreet, several miles away, could bring up his corps. But the battle was out of Lee's hands. The four Confederate divisions at Gettysburg outnumbered the five Union infantry divisions (Confederate divisions averaged 70 percent larger than Union divisions). As Ewell's attack developed, Lee finally told Hill to go in with everything he had.

We next head north on park roads, Reynolds Avenue and Buford Avenue, across open fields where the Union First Corps still held firm as the long, bloody afternoon of July 1 wore on. Our objective is the Eternal Light Peace Memorial crowning Oak Hill where McPherson Ridge and Seminary Ridge come together. This striking monument was dedicated by President Franklin D. Roosevelt to "Peace Eternal in a Nation United" on the seventy-fifth anniversary

Major General Henry Heth.

The Eternal Light Peace Memorial.

of the battle, in July 1938. Attended by more than 1,800 actual Civil War veterans (most in their nineties), this four-day event was the last reunion of Blue and Gray. It culminated a half-century in which reconciliation between old foes was the dominant theme in Civil War memory and in the numerous joint reunions of Union and Confederate veterans.

This uniting of North and South in a renewed American nationalism was a fine thing, to be sure, but all too often it was characterized by forgetting what the war had been about. Absent from these reunions were black Union veterans who, with their white brothers in arms, had fought a war not only to preserve the nation as the United States but also to give that nation a new birth of freedom. And the very spot on which the Eternal Light memorial stands is the location where Major General Robert Rodes's division—the largest in either army, with five brigades—deployed on the early afternoon of July 1 to launch an attack intended to de-stroy that "Nation United."

From the memorial we head southeast on Doubleday Avenue across the Mummasburg Road and past an observation tower, to stop at a stone wall alongside Doubleday Avenue. Here fought part of one Union brigade and all of another commanded by Brigadier General Henry Baxter of New York. Lying behind the stone wall, they rose to pour a devastating fire into an

Alabama brigade, stopping it cold before its attack had gone more than thirty yards. Then Baxter's men jumped to the other side of the wall and almost wiped out a North Carolina brigade commanded by General Alfred Iverson, killing and wounding more than 450 and capturing three hundred. More than a hundred of Iverson's men were buried in a couple of mass graves in a farm field, called Iverson's Pits ever since, where they lay until disinterred in 1873 by Confederate memorial associations and taken to North Carolina for reinterment in local Confederate cemeteries. Gettysburg residents insist that the associations did not find all of the remains, whose spirits rise from Iverson's Pits every July 1 to haunt the battlefield.

One of the Union regiments that fought here was the Eleventh Pennsylvania. Their monument has a small bronze dog at its base on the side away from the road. Like several other Civil War regiments, the Eleventh had a canine mascot, named Sallie. When the Eleventh was finally driven back along with the rest of the Union forces in late afternoon, Sallie stayed behind with the dead of the regiment. She guarded them faithfully through the next four days until the survivors returned to bury them on July 5. Sallie continued with the regiment until she herself was killed in action at the battle of Hatcher's Run in February 1865. For her faithfulness, veterans of the Eleventh honored Sallie when they erected their monument in 1890.

We'll backtrack two hundred yards and climb the observation tower built in the 1890s by the War Department when it administered the battlefield. (The National Park Service, created in 1916, took over Civil War battlefields in 1933.) From here we get a panoramic view of the

Sallie, the mascot and guardian of the Eleventh Pennsylvania Infantry.

first day's battlefield—especially if we are here between November and April when the leaves are off the trees. Looking south we can also see the town of Gettysburg, with Cemetery Hill rising to its south and Culp's Hill to the southeast. On a clear day in winter we can also see, through the bare branches of several oak trees, the Round Tops four miles to the south.

For an understanding of the battle, the most important view from this tower is to the east over the open, flat fields defended by two undersized Eleventh Corps divisions (about six thousand men, smaller than a single Confederate division). Known as the "Dutch Corps" because half its regiments were composed mainly of German-Americans, this corps had been part of the Army of the Potomac for only six months. On May 2 at the battle of Chancellorsville, it had borne the brunt of Stonewall Jackson's flank attack, and had buckled under the onslaught. It buckled again at Gettysburg about 4:00 PM on July 1, setting off a sort of chain reaction in which the Union line of two miles in length caved in from right to left. The First Corps west of town, despite being worn down by hours of fighting, gave ground grudgingly while several Eleventh Corps regiments were again routed. This happened mainly because Jubal Early's division of Ewell's corps had arrived from the northeast on the Harrisburg Road (sometimes called the Heidlersburg Road) a mile east of our observation tower. This route brought them

A haunting view over Iverson's Pits with the stone wall visible in the distance.

Union general Francis Barlow and Confederate general John B. Gordon.

in fortuitously on the right flank of the Eleventh Corps in a whirlwind attack that the brigade on that flank could not withstand.

That brigade was in a division commanded by Brigadier General Francis Barlow, a boyish-looking New York lawyer before the war, who had enlisted in 1861 as a private. Barlow demonstrated extraordinary courage and military aptitude that brought him repeated promotions and a reputation as one of the army's best combat leaders. But July 1, 1863, was not one of his better days. He suffered his second serious wound of the war on what came to be called Barlow's Knoll at the extreme right flank of the Union line, and was left for dead when his troops retreated.

We shall proceed out to Barlow's Knoll along Howard Avenue, lined with Eleventh Corps monuments, to examine yet another of Gettysburg's many myths. This one was probably made up out of whole cloth by Confederate General John B. Gordon, who, like Barlow, was a lawyer (in Georgia) before the war and rose by merit and courage to high command.

Gordon led the brigade that attacked the Barlow's Knoll position and, as he later told the story, spotted Barlow lying wounded and apparently dying. Gordon gave him water and had him carried to a shady spot. Gordon fought on through the rest of the war (wounded six times himself) thinking that Barlow had died. Some fifteen years after the battle, Gordon and Barlow happened to meet at a dinner party in New York, according to Gordon's account in his memoirs. When they were introduced, Gordon supposedly asked, "General, are you related to the Barlow who was killed at Gettysburg?" "Why, I am the man, sir," replied Barlow. "Are you related to the Gordon who killed me?" "I am the man, sir."

This aerial view is from the northwest of Gettysburg. It was taken before the observation tower was built but is from a similar vantage point, with a view of the first day battlefield, the town of Gettysburg, and beyond that Cemetery and Culp's Hills in the distance.

THE FIRST DAY'S FIGHTING

**From the Diary of British Military Observer
Lieutenant Colonel Arthur J. L. Fremantle**

At 2 PM firing became distinctly audible in our front, but although it increased as we progressed, it did not seem to be very heavy. A spy who was with us insisted upon there being "a pretty tidy bunch of bluebellies in or near Gettysburg," and he declared that he was in their society three days ago.

After passing Johnson's division, we came up to a Florida Brigade, which is now in Hill's corps; but as it had formerly served under Longstreet, the men knew him well. Some of them (after the General had passed) called out to their comrades, "Look out for work now, boys, for here's the old bulldog again."

At 3 PM we began to meet wounded men coming to the rear, and the number of these soon increased most rapidly, some hobbling alone, others on stretchers carried

Ambulance wagons.

This famous drawing by Winslow Homer shows a Civil War field surgeon working at the rear of a battle.

by the ambulance corps, and others in the ambulance wagons; many of the latter were stripped nearly naked, and displayed very bad wounds. This spectacle, so revolting to a person unaccustomed to such sights, produced no impression whatever upon the advancing troops, who certainly go under fire with the most perfect nonchalance: they show no enthusiasm or excitement, but the most complete indifference. This is the effect of two years' almost uninterrupted fighting.

We now began to meet Yankee prisoners coming to the rear in considerable numbers: many of them were wounded, but they seemed already to be on excellent terms with their captors, with whom they had commenced swapping canteens, tobacco, &c. Among them was a Pennsylvanian colonel, a miserable object from a wound in his face. In answer to a question, I heard one of them remark, with a laugh, "We're pretty nigh whipped already." We next came to a Confederate soldier carrying a Yankee colour, belonging, I think, to a Pennsylvanian regiment, which he told us he had just captured.

It is a great story, very much in keeping with the sentimental "brother against brother" reconciliationist tradition in vogue when Gordon published his memoirs in 1903 (seven years after Barlow's death). But there is no evidence except Gordon's account to support it. Barlow's letters written at the time mention no such incident. And Gordon's memoirs are in other respects notoriously unreliable. His sword was mightier than his pen—or at least more truthful. Nevertheless, the story has persisted to this day, told by some guides and swallowed by tourists because they want to believe that the Civil War was an unfortunate disagreement between good and honorable men, not a cataclysmic Armageddon. The interpretive marker at Barlow's Knoll quotes from Gordon's account and implicitly endorses it, even though the current park historians do not.

"Christian General" Oliver Otis Howard.

We now continue to the end of Howard Avenue, named for Major General Oliver Otis Howard, commander of the Eleventh Corps. A pious Congregationalist from Maine, a graduate of Bowdoin College as well as of the US Military Academy, Howard was a strong antislavery man. Known as "the Christian General"—a phrase sometimes uttered with disdain by officers who were neither religious nor antislavery—Howard, like his adversary Richard Ewell, had lost a limb earlier in the war—in Howard's case an arm. When he sent two divisions of the Eleventh Corps north of Gettysburg, Howard kept a third small division in reserve on the high ground south of town, known as Cemetery Hill because the town burial ground was located there. Howard fortified the hill with artillery and infantry breastworks as a rallying point for Union troops if they were driven back—a foresighted action that later earned him the official Thanks of Congress. There were those in the army, scornful of Howard because his corps had again been routed, who attributed this award not to Howard's military skill but to his political influence with antislavery Republicans. In any case, the retreating survivors of the First and Eleventh Corps did rally on Cemetery Hill. Ironically, the sign on the cemetery gate stated that "All persons found using firearms on these grounds will be prosecuted with the utmost rigor of the law."

Opposite: The cemetery gates used as a fallback to great effect by Howard.

ROBERT E. LEE TO JEFFERSON DAVIS

OFFICIAL REPORT

Headquarters Army of Northern Virginia, Near Gettysburg, PA,
July 4, 1863

After the rear of the army had crossed the Potomac, the leading corps, under General Ewell, pushed on to Carlisle and York, passing through Chambersburg. The other two corps closed up at the latter place, and soon afterward intelligence was received that the army of General Hooker was advancing. Our whole force was directed to concentrate at Gettysburg, and the corps of Generals Ewell and A. P. Hill reached that place on the 1st July, the former advancing from Carlisle and the latter from Chambersburg.

The two leading divisions of these corps, upon reaching the vicinity of Gettysburg, found the enemy, and attacked him, driving him from the town, which was occupied by our troops. The enemy's loss was heavy, including more than 4,000 prisoners. He took up a strong position in rear of the town, which he immediately began to fortify, and where his re-enforcements joined him.

★ ★ ★

Embattled rebel soldiers.

Brigadier General Alexander Schimmelfennig hid for three days while the Confederates occupied the town.

Almost 9,000 of the 20,500 Union soldiers who fought on July 1 (against 27,500 Confederates) would have no opportunity to use firearms on Cemetery Hill. Nearly 5,500 of them were killed or wounded and 3,500 captured. One of those who didn't make it, however, was neither killed nor captured: Brigadier General Alexander Schimmelfennig, a brigade commander in the Eleventh Corps. Schimmelfennig has achieved minor fame as a Civil War general for reasons he would not have found flattering. A veteran of the Prussian army who immigrated to the United States in 1853, Schimmelfennig saw little action as colonel of the Seventy-fourth Pennsylvania in the war's first year. The Lincoln administration was eager to solidify German-American support for the war effort; one way to do so was to give commissions to visible German-American leaders. Poring over a list of colonels eligible for promotion in the fall of 1862, Lincoln came across Schimmelfennig's name. "The very man!" the president exclaimed. When the secretary of war protested that better-qualified officers were available, Lincoln insisted on Schimmelfennig. "His name will make up for any difference there may be." After Gettysburg, however, Schimmelfennig's name became something of a byword. As his routed brigade retreated through town, Schimmelfennig saved himself from capture by hiding between a woodshed and a pigsty behind a house on Baltimore Street a few blocks south of the main square. There he stayed for the next three days while the Confederates occupied the town, hidden and fed by the woman of the house.

The house (but not the woodshed or pigsty) is still there, identified by one of sixty interpretive markers that are scattered throughout the town to indicate buildings and sites connected with the battle. Virtually every public building and church, as well as several homes, became hospitals during the battle. Considerable fighting took place in Gettysburg's streets during the retreat of the First and Eleventh Corps through the town. A walking tour of these sites, guided by a map available at the town visitor center next to the movie theater on Carlisle Street a block north of the town square, is a must for every visitor who desires a full understanding of the battle and its local impact.

Infantry fire.

One site in town has special significance. As the Eleventh Corps broke in late afternoon, General Howard sent one of the brigades he had kept in reserve into Gettysburg to slow the Confederate advance. They established a defensive position in a brickyard a couple of blocks east of Pennsylvania College (today Gettysburg College) on what is now Coster Avenue, named for the colonel who commanded the brigade. This is the next stop on our tour. We will gather between the monument to the 154th New York and the mural on the side of a warehouse portraying the action at this site.

Amos Humiston was a sergeant in the 154th New York. Thirty-two years old when he enlisted in 1862, Humiston had apprenticed as a harness-maker in his youth. At age twenty, however, he had succumbed to the temptation for adventure and travel as a hand on a whaling ship. After a three-year voyage marked by hardships, dangers, and minimal earnings, he decided that the life of a harness-maker was not so bad after all. He settled down in western New

This wood engraving of a dead soldier clutching a picture of
his children is based on Amos Humiston's story.

York, married, and fathered three children. When war came in 1861, parental responsibilities
prevented him from enlisting. But in 1862 he could no longer hold back.

Here on this spot in the late afternoon of July 1, Humiston was in line with 950 other Union infantrymen facing the onslaught of 2,300 yelling Confederates.

Here on this spot in the late afternoon of July 1, Humiston was in line with 950 other
Union infantrymen facing the onslaught of 2,300 yelling Confederates. Coster's tiny brigade
stemmed the attack for a few vital minutes, buying time for other Eleventh Corps soldiers to
escape, but were soon overwhelmed. Sometime during this firefight, Amos Humiston was
mortally wounded. His body was found a few days later a quarter-mile south of the action,
near today's firehouse on Stratton Street. There stands a monument to Humiston, the only
monument to an individual enlisted man on the battlefield.

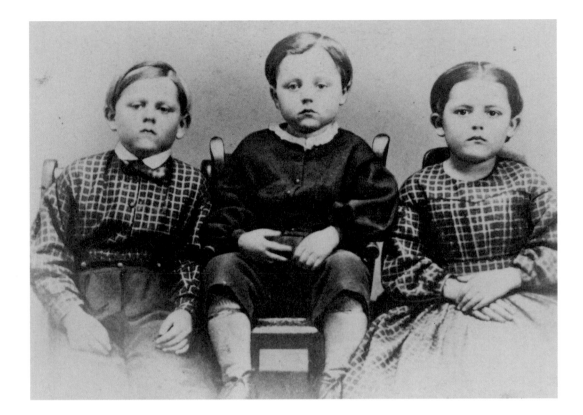

Amos Humiston's children.

When Humiston's body was discovered, it had no identification save an ambrotype of three children (two boys and a girl, ages eight, six, and four) clutched in his hand. It was the last thing he gazed on as he died. "Whose Father Was He?" asked a Philadelphia newspaper. Other papers picked up this question, which soon spread through the North accompanied by woodcut illustrations of the three children. The story plucked at the nation's heartstrings. In November 1863, four months after Amos Humiston's death, a religious weekly carrying the story and picture made its way to Humiston's hometown of Portville, New York, where Philanda Humiston finally learned that she was a widow and her children were fatherless.

That was not the end of the story. Poems and songs about "The Unknown Soldier" and "The Children of the Battlefield" swept the North. *Carte de visite* copies of the ambrotype sold widely. The publicity inspired the founding of a "Homestead Association" to raise money for the establishment in Gettysburg of a home for widows and orphans of Union soldiers. The National Soldiers' Orphan Homestead opened in November 1866 with Philanda Humiston as wardrobe mistress and the three Humiston children as its first residents. Over the eleven years of its existence, the orphanage sheltered and raised hundreds of children. The original buildings still stand on Baltimore Street just north of the entrance to the National Military Cemetery. Today they cater to tourists as the Homestead Lodging Inn and the Soldiers' National Museum.

THE END OF THE FIRST DAY FOR THE CONFEDERATES

LEE'S OFFICIAL REPORT OF OPERATIONS

The enemy gave way on all sides and was driven through Gettysburg with great loss. Major General Reynolds, who was in command, was killed. More than five thousand prisoners, exclusive of a large number of wounded, three pieces of artillery, and several colors were captured.

Among the prisoners were two brigadier generals, one of whom was wounded. Our own loss was heavy, including a number of officers, among whom were Major General Heth, slightly, and Brigadier General Scales, of Pender's division, severely, wounded. The enemy retired to a range of hills south of Gettysburg, where he displayed a strong force of infantry and artillery. It was ascertained from the prisoners that we had been engaged with two corps of the army formerly commanded by General Hooker, and that the remainder of that army under General Meade was approaching Gettysburg. Without information as to its proximity, the strong position which the enemy had assumed could not be attacked without danger of exposing the four divisions present, already weakened and exhausted by a long and bloody struggle, to overwhelming numbers of fresh troops. General Ewell was therefore instructed to carry the hill occupied by the enemy if he found it practicable, but to avoid a general engagement until the arrival of the other divisions of the army which were ordered to hasten forward. He decided to await Johnson's division, which had marched from Carlisle by the road west of the mountains to guard the trains of his corps, and consequently did not reach Gettysburg until a late hour. In the meantime the enemy occupied the point which General Ewell designed to seize, but in what force could not be ascertained

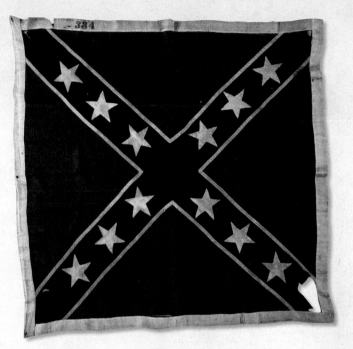

This was the flag of the First Texas Infantry Regiment, who suffered incredible losses at Gettysburg.

owing to the darkness. An intercepted dispatch showed that another corps had halted that afternoon four miles from Gettysburg. Under these circumstances it was decided not to attack until the arrival of Longstreet, two of whose divisions, those of Hood and McLaws encamped about four miles in the rear during the night. Anderson's division of Hill's corps came up after the engagement. It had not been intended to deliver a general battle so far from our base unless attacked, but coming unexpectedly upon the whole Federal Army, to withdraw through the mountains with our extensive trains would have been difficult and dangerous.

★ ★ ★

*Stonewall Jackson being wounded at Chancellorsville;
an injury that would ultimately be fatal.*

*A view of Culp's Hill from Cemetery Hill, two key positions the
Confederates failed to win on the first day of battle.*

By 5:00 PM on July 1 the Confederates appeared to have won a great victory. Gettysburg
was shaping up as another Chancellorsville. Lee was aware, however, that the triumph was
incomplete so long as Union forces held Cemetery Hill and Culp's Hill, to which the remnants
of the First and Eleventh Corps were retreating. Lee also knew that the rest of the Army of
the Potomac must be hurrying toward Gettysburg (indeed, three divisions of the Twelfth and
Third Corps were only a few miles away). Lee thought his best chance to complete the victory
was to gain the hills before Union reinforcements got there.

Lee turned to Ewell, whose two divisions had sustained fewer casualties than Hill's
during the fighting, and whose third division was arriving. Nearly three hours of daylight
remained. Lee gave verbal orders to Ewell to attack Cemetery Hill "if practicable." Ewell
reconnoitered the position, consulted subordinates, and then hesitated. His troops were tired
and disorganized from chasing Yankees through town and rounding up prisoners. They were
suffering from lack of water on a warm day after a long march and intense fighting. Ewell
could see in the fading light that the Union position on Cemetery Hill was formidable. He

HANCOCK TAKES CONTROL AND THE DAY CLOSES

By Abner Doubleday

Hancock being his junior, Howard was naturally unwilling to submit to his authority and, according to Captain Halstead of my staff, who was present, refused to do so. Howard stated in a subsequent account of the battle that he merely regarded General Hancock as a staff officer acting for General Meade. He says "General Hancock greeted me in his usual frank and cordial manner and used these words, 'General Meade has sent me to represent him on the field.' I replied, 'All right, Hancock. This is no time for talking. You take the left of the pike and I will arrange these troops to the right.' I noticed that he sent Wadsworth's division, without consulting me, to the right of the Eleventh Corps to Culp's Hill, but as it was just the thing to do I made no objection." He adds

Major General Winfield S. Hancock.

that Hancock did not really relieve him until 7 PM Hancock, however, denies that he told Howard he was merely acting as a staff officer. He says he assumed absolute command at 3.30 PM I know he rode over to me and told me he was in command of the

Fallen soldiers.

field, and directed me to send a regiment to the right, and I sent Wadsworth's division there, as my regiments were reduced to the size of companies.

Hancock was much pleased with the ridge we were on, as a defensive position, and considered it admirably adapted for a battle-field. Its gentle slopes for artillery, its stone fences and rocky boulders to shelter infantry, and its ragged but commanding eminences on either flank, where far-reaching batteries could be posted, were great advantages. It covered the principal roads to Washington and Baltimore, and its convex shape, enabling troops to reinforce with celerity any point of the line from the centre, or by moving along the chord of this arc, was probably the cause of our final success. The enemy, on the contrary, having a concave order of battle, was obliged to move troops much longer distances to support any part of his line, and could not communicate orders rapidly, nor could the different corps co-operate promptly with each other. It was Hancock's recommendation that caused Meade to concentrate his army on this ridge, but Howard received the thanks of Congress for selecting the position. He, doubtless, did see its advantages, and recommended it to Hancock. The latter immediately took measures to hold it as a battle-ground for the army, while Howard merely used the cemetery as a rallying point for his defeated troops. Hancock occupied all the prominent points, and disposed the little cavalry and infantry he had in such a way as to impress the enemy with the idea that heavy reinforcements had come up. By occupying Culp's Hill, on the right, with Wadsworth's brigade, and posting the cavalry on the left to take up a good deal of space, he made a show of strength not warranted by the facts. Both Hill and Ewell had received some stunning blows during the day, and were disposed to be cautious. They, therefore, did not press forward and take the heights, as they could easily have done at this time, but not so readily after an hour's delay, for then Sickles' corps from Emmetsburg, and Slocum's corps from Two Taverns, began to approach the position. The two rebel divisions of Anderson and Johnson, however, arrived about dusk, which would have still given the enemy a great numerical superiority.

General Lee reached the field before Hancock came, and watched the retreat of the First and Eleventh Corps, and Hancock's movements and dispositions through his field-glass. He was not deceived by this show of force, and sent a recommendation—not an order—to Ewell to follow us up; but Ewell, in the exercise of his discretion as a corps commander, did not do so. He had lost 3,000 men, and both he and Hill were under orders not to bring on a general engagement. In fact they had had all the fighting they desired for the time being. Colonel Campbell Brown, of Ewell's staff, states that the latter was preparing to move forward against the height, when a false report induced him to send Gordon's brigade to reinforce Smith's brigade on his extreme left, to meet a supposed Union advance in that direction.

The absence of these two brigades decided him to wait for the arrival of Johnson's division before taking further action. When the latter came up, Slocum and Sickles were on the ground, and the opportunity for a successful attack had passed.

In sending Hancock forward with such ample powers, Meade virtually appointed him commander-in-chief for the time being, for he was authorized to say where we would fight, and when, and how. In the present instance, in accordance with his recommendation, orders were immediately sent out for the army to concentrate on Cemetery Ridge. Two-thirds of the Third Corps, and all of the Twelfth came up, and by six o'clock the position became tolerably secure.

suspected correctly that newly arriving Union troops were within reinforcing distance. So he decided it was not practicable to attack.

Because the Confederates failed to take Cemetery and Culp's Hills on July 1, Union troops were able to consolidate their position there and on the ridge extending south from Cemetery Hill during the night. General Meade arrived after midnight and decided to stay and fight from this strong defensive position. Ewell's failure to attack has thus been one of the biggest of many ifs concerning the battle of Gettysburg over the years. *If* Jackson had still been alive and in command of this corps, would he have attacked? And *if* he—or Ewell—had done so, would the Confederates have carried the position? Would the battle—and perhaps the war—then have come out differently?

No one can know. Ewell could probably have sent no more than ten or twelve thousand men of his own corps into such an attack, and Lee had told him he could expect no support from any other part of the army. Union forces defending the hills were almost as numerous, dug in and less disorganized than critics of Ewell assume them to have been. General Howard perhaps deserved those Thanks of Congress after all. The best historians of the battle believe that Ewell made the right decision. And as one of those historians put it, "responsibility for the failure of the Confederates to make an all-out assault on Cemetery Hill on July 1 must rest with Lee." He was the commanding general. He was present on the ground. If he wanted an attack, he should have organized and ordered it.

Night fell on a field made hideous by three thousand dead and dying soldiers and the moans of many of the additional seven or eight thousand wounded. The exhausted survivors slept fitfully, unsure of what the morrow might bring.

The calm of night.

DAY TWO

July 2, 1863

BY DAWN of July 2, all of the Army of Northern Virginia had reached Gettysburg except Stuart's cavalry and Major General George Pickett's division plus Brigadier General Evander Law's brigade, both in Longstreet's corps. On the Union side, the large Sixth Corps was still many miles away while the Fifth Corps was nearing the battlefield after an all-night march. Lee was eager to renew the attack, believing that momentum and morale were with his army. From their observation post near the Lutheran Seminary, Lee and Longstreet peered through their binoculars at the Union lines a mile or more away. These lines occupied the high ground south of town in a shape that resembled an upside-down fishhook with its barbed end curving from Culp's Hill through Cemetery Hill and the shank running south along Cemetery Ridge to the eye of the hook on the rocky prominence of Little Round Top. This was

On July 2, 1863, the second day of Gettysburg, the First Minnesota played a critical role in preventing Confederate forces from overtaking the Union line on Cemetery Ridge. Of the 262 men to charge into battle, only 47 answered roll call that night. Their efforts are memorialized in this painting by Don Troiani.

Longstreet commanding soldiers during the second day.

a strong position. It followed high ground except for a half-mile just north of Little Round Top, where the ridge dipped into a swale commanded by higher ground in a peach orchard along the Emmitsburg Road nearly a mile to the west. The convex shape of the Union line, with its flanks only two miles apart, enabled troops to be shifted quickly from one place to another to reinforce weak spots. By contrast, the much longer concave exterior lines held by the Confederates made communication between the widely separated flanks slow and difficult.

A master of defensive tactics, Longstreet recognized the strength of the Union position. Some Southern officers considered Longstreet ponderous, stubborn, and phlegmatic. But in reality he was reflective and sagacious. He recognized better than some of his colleagues that courage and dash could not overcome determined defenders armed with rifled muskets. These weapons had an accurate range three times greater than the smoothbore muskets of the Napoleonic Wars or the Mexican War, in which many senior Civil War commanders (including Longstreet) had fought.

After studying the Union position on the morning of July 2, Longstreet concluded that an attack had little chance of success. He urged Lee to move south (toward Washington) and find some good defensive terrain. This maneuver, said Longstreet, would compel Meade to attack the Confederates, who could stand on the defensive and repeat the victories of Second Manassas and Fredericksburg. But Lee's blood was up. He rejected the advice. The model of a successful battle most vivid in his mind was Chancellorsville, just two months earlier. Courage and dash—plus some dazzling tactical maneuvers by Lee and Jackson—had enabled them to overcome superior numbers and win that battle by attacking, not by fighting on the defensive. Longstreet had not been at Chancellorsville. With Pickett's and Major General John Bell Hood's divisions, he had been operating against Union forces in the Norfolk-Suffolk region of Virginia. Nor had Longstreet arrived at Gettysburg on July 1 in time to see Hill's and Ewell's divisions drive the enemy pell-mell through the town.

Opposite: This detailed map shows the topography of Gettysburg.

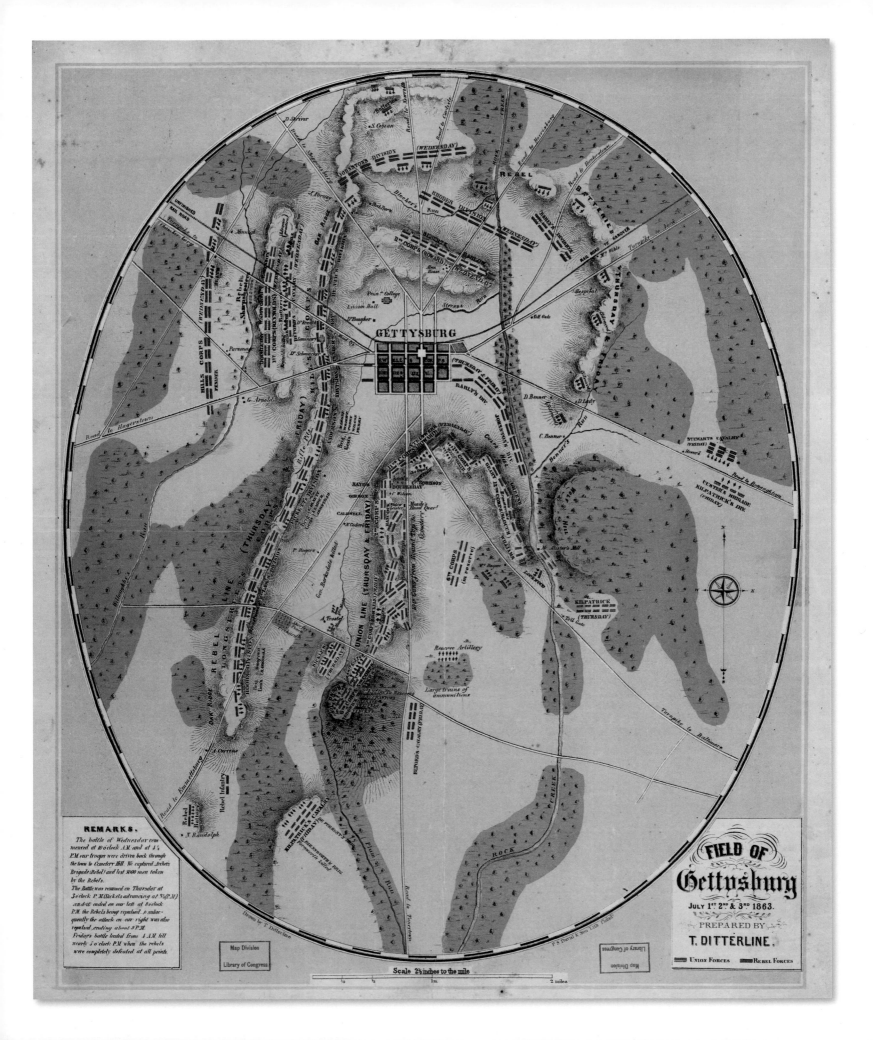

REMARKS.

The battle of Wednesday commenced at 10 o'clock A.M. and at 4 ½ P.M. our troops were driven back through the town to Cemetery Hill. We captured Archer's Brigade (Rebel) and lost 3000 men taken by the Rebels.

The Battle was resumed on Thursday at 3 o'clock P.M Sickels advancing at 3 ½ P.M and it ended on our left at 5 o'clock P.M. the Rebels being repulsed. subsequently the attack on our right was also repulsed, ending about 9 P.M.

Friday's battle lasted from 4 A.M. till nearly 5 o'clock P.M when the rebels were completely defeated at all points.

Drawn by T. Ditterline.

P. S. Duval & Son Lith. Philad.ª

Map Division
Library of Congress

Library of Congress
Map Division

Scale 2 ½ inches to the mile

2 miles

FIELD OF
Gettysburg
JULY 1ST 2ND & 3RD 1863.
PREPARED BY
T. DITTERLINE.

— UNION FORCES   — REBEL FORCES

HOOD RACES TO THE BATTLE

HOOD'S OFFICIAL REPORT

While lying in camp near Chambersburg information was received that Hill and Ewell were about to come into contact with the enemy near Gettysburg. My troops, together with McLaws's division, were at once put in motion upon the most direct road to that point, which we reached after a hard march at or before sunrise on July 2. So imperative had been our orders to hasten forward with all possible speed that on the march my troops were allowed to halt and rest only about two hours during the night from the 1st to the 2d of July.

★ ★ ★

General John Bell Hood.

A unique topographical map of the battle.

Confederate success on July 1 had confirmed Lee's belief in the invincibility of his men. Their morale was high, despite the seven thousand casualties they had sustained. According to Colonel Arthur Fremantle, a British observer accompanying the Army of Northern Virginia, the Confederates were eager to attack an enemy "they had beaten so constantly" and for whose fighting capacity they felt "profound contempt." They might regard the move that Longstreet suggested as a retreat, and lose their edge. With limited supplies and a vulnerable line of communications to Virginia, Lee could not stay in Pennsylvania indefinitely. He had come there to win a battle; he intended to do so that day. Pointing toward Cemetery Hill, he said to Longstreet, "The enemy is there, and I am going to attack him there." Longstreet replied, "If he is there, it will be because he is anxious that we should attack him; a good reason, in my judgment, for not doing so." But Lee had made up his mind. Longstreet turned away sadly, as he wrote years later, with a conviction of impending disaster.

Lee's intent was to attack both Union flanks on July 2. But after looking over the position on Culp's Hill and Cemetery Hill, he agreed with Ewell that the Union right was too strong. Lee therefore ordered Longstreet to take his two divisions (the third, Pickett's, would not arrive in time) plus Hill's one division that had not fought the previous day and attack the Union left. Ewell would demonstrate against the enemy in his front, and convert the demonstration into an attack if Meade weakened that flank to reinforce his left against Longstreet's assault.

An authentic Confederate flag.

Longstreet took a long time getting his troops into position for the attack. A large part of the delay was not his fault. The shortage of cavalry had made it difficult to scout a route to the jump-off point. (Stuart's troopers were finally on their way to Gettysburg, but would not get there until evening.) Because the Confederates did not want to telegraph the point of attack, Longstreet had to countermarch several miles after discovering that the original approach road could be seen from a Union signal station on Little Round Top.

Part of Longstreet's slowness on July 2 may also have resulted from a lack of enthusiasm for the attack he had been ordered to make. After the war, he became a target of withering criticism from Virginians who dominated the writing of Confederate history. They accused him of insubordination and tardiness at Gettysburg. They held him responsible for losing the battle—and, by implication, the war. But some of this criticism was self-serving, intended to shield Lee and other Virginians (chiefly Ewell and Stuart) from blame. In the eyes of unreconstructed Southern whites, Longstreet also made the mistake of urging them to accept the results of the war. Even worse, he became a Republican and received a federal appointment from President Ulysses S. Grant, a friend of Longstreet from their days together at West Point.

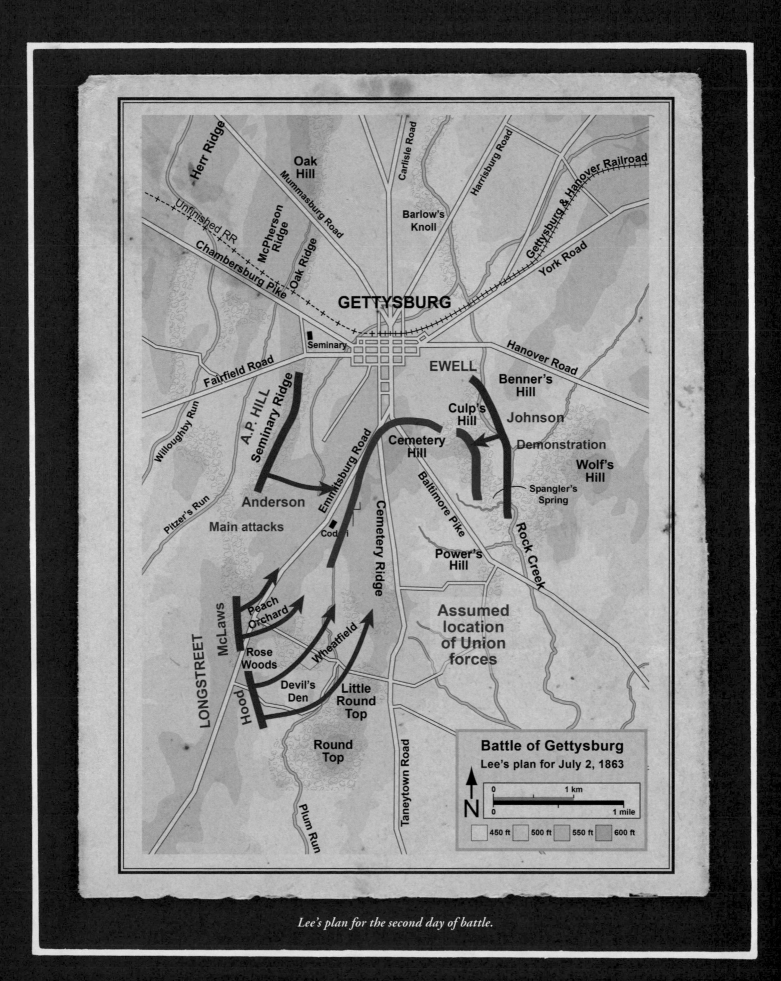

Lee's plan for the second day of battle.

MORNING OF THE SECOND DAY

By James Longstreet

The stars were shining brightly on the morning of the 2d when I reported at General Lee's head-quarters and asked for orders. After a time Generals McLaws and Hood, with their staffs, rode up, and at sunrise their commands filed off the road to the right and rested. The Washington Artillery was with them, and about nine o'clock, after an all-night march, Alexander's batteries were up as far as Willoughby's Run, where he parked and fed, and rode to head-quarters to report.

As indicated by these movements, General Lee was not ready with his plans. He had not heard from his cavalry, nor of the movements of the enemy further than the information from a despatch captured during the night, that the Fifth Corps was in camp about five miles from Gettysburg, and the Twelfth Corps was reported near Culp's Hill. As soon as it was light enough to see, however, the enemy was found in position on his formidable heights awaiting us.

A postcard from the 1930s promoting Lee's headquarters at Gettysburg.

A view down West Confederate Avenue, looking south from the observation tower.

We will leave Longstreet's troops for a while and proceed south along Seminary Ridge on the park road called West Confederate Avenue, which follows part of the Confederate line of July 2 and 3. Along the way we will see many cannons and monuments of various kinds—as indeed we have been seeing since the beginning of our tour. The numbers of monuments and cannons and other physical artifacts of the battle and its commemoration are far greater than at any other battlefield. There are something like 1,400 monuments and markers of various sorts, and almost four hundred cannons. The carriages of the latter are replicas, but most of the guns themselves actually date from the war, and some of them were at Gettysburg in 1863. They are placed today in the approximate position where they, or ones like them, fought during the battle (there were more than four hundred cannons with the two armies at Gettysburg).

About a hundred battery markers today indicate the principal locations of each six- or four-gun artillery battery during the battle. Other official bronze markers (placed by the War Department a century ago, when it administered the battlefield) stand where each of the seventy Union and fifty-six Confederate brigades fought. Union brigade markers have a square base, and Confederate markers a round base. Granite markers with a bronze tablet stand at or near the command sites of the twenty-two Union divisions (2,500 to 5,000 men) and ten Confederate divisions (5,500 to 8,000 men). Similar corps markers indicate the headquarters of the seven Union infantry and one cavalry corps and the three Confederate infantry corps

Left: This brigade marker indicates the location of Longstreet's headquarters.
Right: A brigade headquarters monument erected by the War Department.

and one cavalry division. These markers describe the actions and casualties of those units during the battle.

The monuments of greatest interest to most visitors are those erected by the veterans (or their descendants) of many Union regiments and a few Confederate regiments that fought at Gettysburg, or by their states. Conforming to no single pattern or material or size, regimental monuments commemorate the actions and casualties of those regiments during the battle. Sometimes they list all the battles (and casualties) of the regiment during the entire war. Union regimental associations began placing monuments in the 1880s—forty-seven in 1885 alone—and by 1904 there were some 360 regimental and state monuments on the battlefield, nearly all of them Union. Many Northern states appropriated five hundred dollars or more to supplement private contributions for regimental monuments, and appropriated larger sums for the imposing state monuments.

Few Southern veterans or states had the resources or interest to commemorate a battle they had lost. Beginning with Virginia in 1917, however, Southern states and Confederate heritage groups began placing monuments, some of them of impressive size and beauty. My favorite, from an aesthetic standpoint, is the Virginia monument at midpoint on West Confederate Avenue. By one count, however, in the year 2000 there were 472 Union regimental and state monuments in the park, compared with only twenty-seven such Confederate monuments.

This modern-looking monument for the 90th Pennsylvania was actually erected in 1888.
Known as the Granite Tree Monument, it is one of the most unique in Gettysburg.

ON LONGSTREET'S ASSAULT

By Abner Doubleday

There has been a great deal of bitter discussion between Longstreet, Fitz Lee, Early, Wilcox, and others as to whether Lee did or did not order an attack to take place at 9 AM, and as to whether Longstreet was dilatory, and to blame for not making it. When a battle is lost there is always an inquest, and a natural desire on the part of each general to lay the blame on somebody else's shoulders. Longstreet waited until noon for Law's brigade to come up, and afterward there was a good

deal of marching and countermarching to avoid being seen by our troops. There was undoubtedly too much delay. The fact is, Longstreet saw we had a strong position and was not well pleased at the duty assigned him, for he thought it more than probable his attempt would fail. He had urged Lee to take up a position where Meade would be forced to attack him, and was not in very good humor to find his advice disregarded. The rebel commander, however, finding the Army of the Potomac in front of him, having unbounded confidence in his troops, and elated by the success of the first day's fight, believed he could gain a great victory then and there, and end the war, and determined to attempt it. He was sick of these endless delays and constant sacrifices, and hoped one strong sword-thrust would slay his opponent, and enable the South to crown herself queen of the North American continent.

This lithograph shows Lee and his generals. Fitz Lee is in the back row, third from the left. Early is on horseback to the left of Lee, who is shown in center. Longstreet is on horseback to the immediate right of Lee.

A detail shot of the base of the Virginia monument.

Our next stop will be at one of those Confederate monuments—and one of the park's newest—the equestrian statue of Longstreet near the Pitzer Woods sign on West Confederate Avenue, several hundred yards north of the observation tower visible in the distance. This is the first monument to Longstreet anywhere—testimony to his lack of popularity in the South. And for many years the North Carolina branch of the Sons of Confederate Veterans, which launched the drive for a Longstreet monument with the slogan "It's About Time," had difficulty raising funds. With the support of other groups (some in the North), they finally succeeded, and the monument was dedicated before a crowd of four thousand people on July 3, 1998, the 135th anniversary of the battle's final day.

It *is* about time for Longstreet to get his due. Historians have long recognized his abilities and have absolved him of responsibility for "losing" Gettysburg. Michael Shaara's novel *The Killer Angels* (1974) and the 1993 movie *Gettysburg* based on the novel have given Longstreet's role at Gettysburg high and favorable visibility. Nevertheless, his monument has not escaped controversy. The careful observer will note that one hoof of the horse is off the ground. Yet Longstreet was not wounded in the battle, so the monument does not conform to the Gettysburg pattern. The sculptor wanted to portray Longstreet as reining in his galloping horse as he arrives to deal with a crisis. He received permission from the Park Service to show the left front hoof of the horse in the air as its rider pulls back the reins. Fair enough. The sculptor also placed the monument at ground level instead of on a pedestal, for greater realism.

The Longstreet equestrian monument.

Many visitors like that notion. But in a milieu where all of the other equestrian statues of generals are on pedestals, conveying an idea of heroic stature, the down-to-earth Longstreet seems to some observers to be somehow demeaned.

The careful observer will note that one hoof of the horse is off the ground.

And almost everyone notices that the horse is too small in comparison with the man. Curiously, that was intentional. I dropped in on the sculptor one day when he was working on the clay model for this bronze sculpture. He explained that Longstreet was full size and the horse four-fifths size so that when one looked up at the monument on its pedestal, the proportions would appear correct. But then why put it at ground level? If that was a later idea, why not then make the horse full size? There is a mystery here that no one has yet explained to me. In any event, a colleague commented that the Virginian Jubal Early, an unreconstructed rebel who led the postwar campaign against Longstreet's reputation, would have selected precisely this kind of monument for Longstreet.

GENERAL JEB STUART ARRIVES

OFFICIAL BATTLE REPORT BY JEB STUART

Reaching Dover, PA, on the morning of July 1, I was unable to find our forces. The most I could learn was that General Early had marched his division in the direction of Shippensburg, which the best information I could get seemed to indicate as the point of concentration of our troops.

After as little rest as was compatible with the exhausted condition of the command, we pushed on for Carlisle, where we hoped to find a portion of the army. I arrived before that village, by way of Dillsburg, in the afternoon. Our rations were entirely out. I desired to levy a contribution on the inhabitants for rations, but was informed before reaching it that it was held by a considerable force of militia (infantry and artillery), who were concealed in the buildings, with the view to entrap me upon my entrance into the town. They were frustrated in their intention, and although very peaceable in external aspect, I soon found the information I had received was correct. I disliked to subject the town to the consequences of attack; at the same time it was essential to us to procure rations. I therefore directed General Lee to send in a flag of truce, demanding unconditional surrender or bombardment. This was refused. I placed artillery in position commanding the town, took possession of the main avenues to the place, and repeated the demand. It was again refused, and I was forced to the alternative of shelling the place.

Although the houses were used by their sharpshooters while firing on our men, not a building was fired excepting the United States cavalry barracks, which were burned by my order, the place having resisted my advance instead of peaceable surrender, as in the case of General Ewell. General Fitz. Lee's brigade was charged with the duty of investing the place, the remaining brigades following at considerable intervals from Dover. Maj. Gen. W. F. Smith was in command of the forces in Carlisle. The only obstacle to the enforcement of my threat was the scarcity of artillery ammunition.

Stuart's forces were exhausted from their long marches.

The whereabouts of our army was still a mystery; but, during the night, I received a dispatch from General Lee (in answer to one sent by Major Venable from Dover, on Early's trail), that the army was at Gettysburg, and had been engaged on this day (July 1) with the enemy's advance. I instantly dispatched to Hampton to move 10 miles that night on the road to Gettysburg, and gave orders to the other brigades, with a view to reaching Gettysburg early the next day, and started myself that night.

My advance reached Gettysburg July 2, just in time to thwart a move of the enemy's cavalry upon our rear by way of Hunterstown. After a fierce engagement, in which Hampton's brigade performed gallant service, a series of charges compelling the enemy to leave the field and abandon his purpose. I took my position that day on the York and Heidlersburg roads, on the left wing of the Army of Northern Virginia.

★ ★ ★

Longstreet's attack on the left-center Union line.

A stereo card print of the fighting in the Peach Orchard.

We must now cast our imagination back to 1863. It is almost 4:00 PM on July 2 of that year. Longstreet's troops have finally arrived and deployed for attack after their roundabout march of several miles to avoid detection from enemy observers on Little Round Top. One of Longstreet's brigades, Alabamians commanded by Evander Law, had marched twenty-five miles since breaking camp at 1:00 AM. Our walk will take us only four-tenths of a mile south from the Longstreet monument to climb the observation tower, which is located near the site of Longstreet's headquarters during the ensuing attack. From the tower we get a panoramic view of the southern half of the battlefield, and can even see the Eternal Light Peace Memorial more than three miles to the north. Behind us as we face to the east is the Eisenhower National Historic Site, a beautiful farm to which Dwight Eisenhower retired after his presidency. Tickets to visit the farm can be obtained at the park visitor center.

But our concern is with the events that took place in our front during the three hours after 4:00 PM on July 2, 1863—some of the most intense fighting and concentrated carnage of the whole Civil War. One-third of a mile due east is the famous Peach Orchard. The peach trees there today cover less than half the acreage of its historic predecessor. A quarter-mile south of the orchard we see the surviving buildings of the Rose farm, where some of the most famous

Big Round Top on the left and Little Round Top on the right.

photographs of Confederate soldiers killed in the battle were taken. Visible a half-mile east of the Peach Orchard is the Trostle farm, where the most famous wartime photographs of dead artillery horses were taken.

Beyond the woods behind the Rose farm was the Wheatfield, a thirty-two-acre field over which attacks and counterattacks surged back and forth, leaving so many dead and wounded that one soldier afterward said (no doubt with some exaggeration) that he could have walked over it without touching the ground. Beyond the Wheatfield, a mile southeast of our tower, is Devil's Den, a geological marvel of huge basalt boulders tumbled together to form a strong defensive position that Confederates nevertheless managed to capture. From our tower the woods block our view of the Wheatfield and Devil's Den. But another five hundred yards east of Devil's Den we can see the steep and rocky rise of Little Round Top, open and mostly free of trees on its western face. Just south of Little Round Top towers Big Round Top, more than a hundred feet higher, rugged and wooded today as it was in 1863.

When one of Lee's staff officers had scouted the Union position in this vicinity early that morning, he had spotted its left flank on Little Round Top and the line running north through low ground a half-mile east of the Wheatfield before gradually rising to Cemetery Ridge. But when Longstreet deployed for attack that afternoon, scouts reported that the Union line had moved forward with its left flank now in Devil's Den, an apex in the Peach Orchard, and a division deployed for a half-mile north along the Emmitsburg Road (today's Business Route 15) and disconnected from the rest of the Union line back on Cemetery Ridge. What had happened? Thereby hangs a tale that spawned one of the sharpest controversies on the Union side at Gettysburg.

At the center of this controversy was Major General Daniel E. Sickles, commander of the Union Third Corps holding the south end of Cemetery Ridge with its left flank on Little Round Top. At least that was where they were supposed to be. In a war with many colorful characters, Sickles stood out with the gaudiest hues. He was the only nonprofessional (not a West Point graduate) corps commander in either army. A New York lawyer and politician, he was prominent in the Tammany Hall political machine during the 1850s. He was also a notorious womanizer, despite the beauty and charms of his wife, Teresa. Elected to Congress in 1856, Sickles may have regretted that he ever came to Washington. His wife began an affair there with Philip Barton Key, son of the composer of "The Star-Spangled Banner." When Sickles finally discovered what was going on, in February 1859, he seized a revolver and shot Key dead in Lafayette Park, directly across Pennsylvania Avenue from the White House.

The sensational trial ended in Sickles's acquittal. One of his attorneys was Edwin M. Stanton, who became Lincoln's secretary of war in 1862. Stanton argued for acquittal on grounds of temporary insanity—the first use of that defense in the history of American jurisprudence. This argument may have helped sway the jury, but the real reason they acquitted Sickles was the "unwritten law" that justified a husband's murder of his wife's lover. Although freed under the law, Sickles was shunned by polite society. To recoup his

Confederate dead on the Rose farm, looking toward the orchard.

Dead artillery horses in front of Trostle's farmhouse.

This Harper's Weekly *illustration was captioned "Homicide of P. Barton Key by Hon. Daniel E. Sickles, at Washington on Sunday, February 27, 1859."*

standing, he raised a brigade (four regiments) in New York City when the war broke out, and was rewarded with appointment as brigadier general to command the brigade.

The Confederates had promptly moved artillery to Hazel Grove, from where they dominated Union guns on lower ground . . .

Demonstrating military ability despite no training or previous experience, Sickles hitched his star to General Joseph Hooker, who had charge of the Third Corps for a time in 1862–63. Sickles won promotion to division command and then took over the corps when Hooker became army commander in January 1863. Although he was Hooker's protégé, he had opposed the commander's decision to pull Sickles back from the high ground at Hazel Grove to straighten Union lines during the battle of Chancellorsville. The Confederates had promptly moved artillery to Hazel Grove, from where they dominated Union guns on lower ground and played a key role in the Southern victory—or at least that was how Sickles saw it.

LONGSTREET ON SICKLES AND THE SECOND DAY OF GETTYSBURG

By James Longstreet

Major General Daniel E. Sickles.

At the opening of the fight, General Meade was with General Sickles discussing the feasibility of moving the Third Corps back to the line originally assigned for it, but the discussion was cut short by the opening of the Confederate battle. If that opening had been delayed thirty or forty minutes the corps would have been drawn back to the general line, and my first deployment would have enveloped Little Round Top and carried it before it could have been strongly manned, and General Meade would have drawn off to his line selected behind Pipe Creek. The point should have been that the battle was opened too soon.

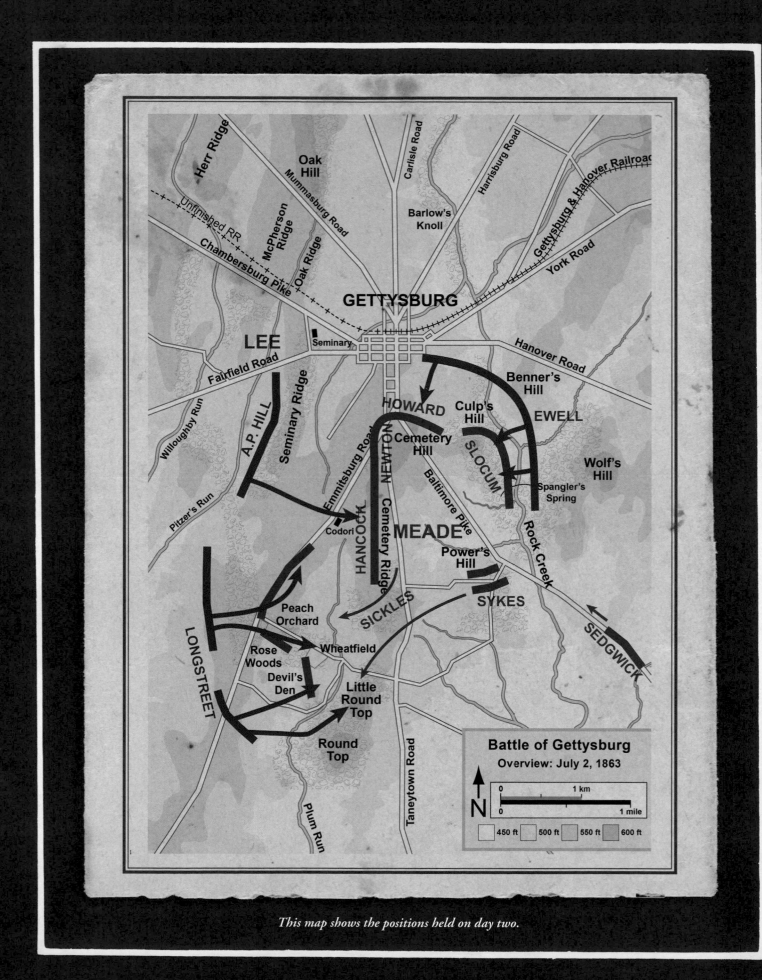

This map shows the positions held on day two.

At Gettysburg he was determined not to let the same thing happen again. Sickles was unhappy about the vulnerability of his position just north of Little Round Top, which was commanded by the higher ground in the Peach Orchard almost a mile to the west. When skirmishers discovered signs of Confederate activity in his front in early afternoon, Sickles feared that the enemy would occupy the Peach Orchard and turn it into another Hazel Grove. Therefore, without notifying Meade—indeed, in violation of Meade's orders—Sickles moved his two divisions forward to take up an inverted V position with its apex at the Peach Orchard.

For the remaining fifty-one years of his life, Sickles insisted that his action saved the Union army at Gettysburg. If so, it was at the cost of 4,200 casualties (including Sickles, who lost a leg) to his ten-thousand-man corps. But Sickles's critics—who have been legion—insisted that he almost lost the battle because his forward move left Little Round Top undefended. If the Confederates had managed to seize that hill, they could have dominated the whole Union position and perhaps have rolled up the exposed flank on Cemetery Ridge.

The argument will never be settled. When we go forward to the Peach Orchard and look east toward the position that Sickles had been ordered to hold, it will become clear why he considered the Peach Orchard a dominant site. When we later ascend Little Round Top, it will become even more clear why this rocky elevation was an even more crucial position. In any event, by the time Meade learned what Sickles had done, it was too late to order him back to the original line.

The Peach Orchard today.

EMMITSBURG ROAD AND THE ROUND TOPS

OFFICIAL BATTLE REPORT BY JOHN BELL HOOD TO JAMES LONGSTREET

The reconnoissance [sic] by my Texas scouts and the development of the Federal lines were effected in a very short space of time; in truth, shorter than I have taken to recall and jot down these facts, although the scenes and events of that day are as clear to my mind as if the great battle had been fought yesterday. I was in possession of these important facts so shortly after reaching the Emmettsburg road, that I considered it my duty to report to you at once my opinion, that it was unwise to attack up the Emmettsburg road, as ordered, and to urge that you allow me to turn Round Top and attack the enemy in flank and rear. Accordingly, I dispatched a staff officer bearing to you my request to be allowed to make the proposed movement on account of the above stated reasons. Your reply was quickly received: "General Lee's orders are to attack up the Emmettsburg road." I sent another officer to say that I feared nothing could be accomplished by such an attack, and renewed my request to turn Round Top. Again your answer was: "General Lee's orders are to attack up the Emmettsburg road."

This view from Emmitsburg Road shows the pillar monument for the state of Vermont with the pavilion monument for the state of Pennsylvania (the largest monument in the park) behind it.

During this interim I had continued the use of the batteries upon the enemy, and had become more and more convinced that the Federal line extended to Round Top, and that I could not reasonably hope to accomplish much by the attack as ordered. In fact it seemed to me the enemy occupied a position by nature so strong—I may say impregnable—that, independent of their flank fire, they could easily repel our attack by merely throwing and rolling stones down the mountain side as we approached.

A third time I dispatched one of my staff to explain fully in regard to the situation, and to suggest that you had better come and look for yourself. I selected, in this instance, my adjutant general, Colonel Harry Sellers, whom you know to be not only an officer of great courage, but also of marked ability. Colonel Sellers returned with the same message: "General Lee's orders are to attack up the Emmettsburg road." Almost simultaneously, Colonel Fairfax, of your staff, rode up and repeated the above orders. After this urgent protest against entering into battle at Gettysburg according to instructions—which protest is the first and only one I ever made during my entire military career—I ordered my line to advance and make the assault.

As my troops were moving forward, you rode up in person; a brief conversation passed between us, during which I again expressed the fears above mentioned, and regret at not being allowed to attack in flank around Round Top. You answered to this effect: "We must obey the orders of General Lee." I then rode forward with my line under a heavy fire. In about twenty minutes after reaching the peach orchard I was severely wounded in the arm, and borne from the field. With this wound terminated my participation in this great battle. As I was borne off on a litter to the rear, I could but experience deep distress of mind and heart at the thought of the inevitable fate of my brave fellow soldiers, who formed one of the grandest divisions of that world renowned army; and I shall ever believe that had I been permitted to turn Round Top mountain, we would not only have gained that position, but have been able finally to route the enemy.

★ ★ ★

A panoramic view of Devil's Den.

At 4:00 PM Longstreet's attack exploded from the woods along Warfield and Seminary Ridges. From right to left, one brigade after another, nineteen thousand rebels (including three brigades of A. P. Hill's corps) hit the Yankees at the Rose farm, the Wheatfield, Devil's Den, the Peach Orchard, and the Trostle farm. After bitter, costly fighting they captured each of these famous locales. Mounted on his horse while watching the action from his headquarters at the Trostle farm, Sickles felt a sharp pain in his right leg and looked down to see it hanging in shreds from his thigh, almost severed by a cannonball. Although Sickles remained conscious, a rumor began to spread among his troops that he was dead. To forestall a panic, Sickles had an aide light a cigar and stick it in his mouth. He puffed away jauntily as he was carried to the rear on a stretcher. His amputated leg was preserved in formaldehyde at a medical laboratory in Washington, where in later years Sickles would take visitors to see it. We can visit his shinbone today at the Museum of Health and Medicine in Washington.

Descending from the observation tower, we will make our way to the Peach Orchard. From there a stroll of half a mile south will take us to the Rose farm and the woods beyond. A half-mile to the east of the Peach Orchard will bring us to the Wheatfield, and a half-mile to the northeast to the Trostle farm. At each place, interpretive markers and numerous monuments explain the actions that occurred there. A further stroll a quarter-mile south of the Wheatfield will take us to the fantastic landscape at Devil's Den, and more markers and monuments. After three hours of fighting in these places, the ground was covered with

A dead Confederate soldier in Devil's Den.

at least eight thousand dead and wounded soldiers, about evenly divided between blue and gray. Meade and his subordinates skillfully fed units from the Fifth and Second Corps into the battle, using the interior lines that made the Union position so strong. These reinforcements counterattacked to regain some of the positions lost by Sickles's corps and to prevent a Confederate breakthrough on Cemetery Ridge. But when dusk turned into darkness at about 8:00 PM, the Confederates still held Devil's Den, the Wheatfield, the Peach Orchard, and the Trostle farm.

The Alabama state monument.

Just across the road north of the Peach Orchard is the foundation of a farmhouse. In 1863 John and Mary Wentz, both in their seventies, lived in this house. Their son Henry, a carriage-maker, had moved to Martinsburg, Virginia (now West Virginia), several years before the war. In 1862 he enlisted in a Virginia artillery battery and fought at Gettysburg with that unit. Soon after the battle a legend arose that "Captain" Wentz had commanded a battery that shelled his parents' house after Wentz had sent them to the cellar to protect them. Then he was killed in a Union counterattack and buried in his father's backyard, his parents refusing even to look at their apostate rebel son. An enthralling story, but there is not a bit of truth to it. Henry Wentz was a sergeant, not a captain; he was nowhere near the house during the battle; and he survived both the battle and the war.

From the Peach Orchard we will head south on the Emmitsburg Road and bear left onto South Confederate Avenue. One-third of a mile farther on the right is the Alabama state monument, which marks the position from which Evander Law's tired and thirsty brigade led off Longstreet's attack. Looking to the northeast we can see the highest part of Little Round Top looming above the intervening woods. In 1863 most of those woods were not there, and the five Alabama plus two Texas regiments would have been visible from Little Round Top as they moved across the open fields toward the Round Tops in late afternoon. If the Park Service carries out its restoration plans, eighty-eight acres of woods that were not there then will be gone again by the time this book appears. Maybe.

In 1863 these troops were spotted from Little Round Top. When Longstreet's assault began, the only Union soldiers at this key position were a handful of signal corpsmen. Meade had sent the army's chief of engineers, Brigadier General Gouverneur K. Warren, to check on affairs at Little Round Top. As Warren later told it, he asked a Union cannoneer to send a shot toward a woodlot a mile away. Confederate soldiers concealed there jerked suddenly, and Warren saw the glint of sunlight reflected from their rifle barrels. The story sounds rather fanciful, especially since the late-afternoon sun was

This photochrom—a colorized print from a black-and-white negative—shows the monument to Brigadier General Warren on top of Little Round Top, looking out over the Wheatfield.

The Twentieth Maine monument.

behind the Confederates. More likely the signalmen told Warren there were Confederate troops across the way, and he soon saw them moving out from the treeline. Hurriedly sending orders for reinforcements to double-time to Little Round Top, Warren earned his niche in history.

The brigade that came was commanded by Pennsylvanian Strong Vincent, recently promoted from colonel to brigadier general. As millions of readers and viewers of the novel *The Killer Angels* and the movie *Gettysburg* know, one of the regiments in this brigade was the Twentieth Maine, commanded by Colonel Joshua Lawrence Chamberlain, ex-professor of rhetoric and modern languages at Bowdoin College. Vincent posted the Twentieth at the left of his four-regiment brigade, getting the whole brigade in position just minutes before enemy regiments began their assault on Little Round Top.

Vincent posted the Twentieth at the left of his four-regiment brigade, getting the whole brigade in position just minutes before enemy regiments began their assault on Little Round Top.

We can easily find our way to the Twentieth Maine monument, about 250 yards southeast of the Little Round Top parking area. When I first visited Gettysburg in the 1960s, scarcely any tourist knew about the Twentieth Maine, and few ever saw its monument, which is tucked away from the others that are back on the west face of Little Round Top. After *The Killer Angels* was published in 1974 and won the Pulitzer Prize, the Park Service put up a sign pointing to the regiment's monument and position. After Ken Burns's video documentary *The Civil War* in 1990, which prominently featured Chamberlain, and the movie *Gettysburg* in 1993, two interpretive markers, more directional signs, a paved walkway, and an auxiliary parking lot just below the monument materialized. Now this site is the most heavily visited in the Park.

Joshua Lawrence Chamberlain became an iconic figure in the 1990s. More people on the tours I have led want to see where he fought than anything else. Powerful emotions have

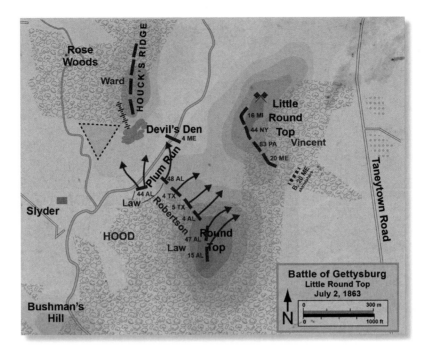

The initial attack on Little Round Top.

gripped some of them as they stared at the simple stone and bronze monument and their imaginations drifted back to those desperate moments about 7:00 PM on that July 2. I remember one such occasion in particular. In April 1987 I took a group of Princeton students on a tour of the battlefield, as I have done many times. This year one of those students had written her senior thesis on Chamberlain, but had never before actually been to Gettysburg. As we came to the place where the Twentieth Maine fought, she could no longer hold back the tears. Nor could the rest of us. Although I have experienced other powerful emotions while walking Civil War battlefields, none has ever matched that April day in 1987. The world has little noted what I said there, but it can never forget what they did there.

Several of Chamberlain's ancestors had fought in the American Revolution. His father had wanted young Lawrence (as his family called him) to pursue a military career. But his mother wanted him to become a clergyman. She seemed to have gotten her way; Lawrence graduated Phi Beta Kappa from Bowdoin and earned a BD from Bangor Theological Seminary. In 1855 he accepted a professorship at Bowdoin, succeeding Calvin Stowe, whose wife, Harriet Beecher Stowe, had written *Uncle Tom's Cabin* while Chamberlain was a student there. Chamberlain knew Mrs. Stowe, and like thousands of others he was moved by her novel to work for the abolition of slavery.

In 1862 he got his chance. Although thirty-three years old and the father of three children, he considered it his duty to fight for Union and freedom. To dissuade him, Bowdoin offered him a two-year sabbatical to study in Europe. Instead, Chamberlain went to the state capital and accepted a commission in the newly organized Twentieth Maine. He was probably the only officer in either army who could read seven foreign languages—these seven, at least: Greek, Latin, Arabic, Hebrew, Syriac, French, and German.

ON LITTLE ROUND TOP

OFFICIAL REPORT BY
JOSHUA LAWRENCE CHAMBERLAIN

The artillery fire on our position had meanwhile been constant and heavy, but my formation was scarcely complete when the artillery was replaced by a vigorous infantry assault upon the center of our brigade to my right, but it very soon involved the right of my regiment and gradually extended along my entire front. The action was quite sharp and at close quarters.

In the midst of this, an officer from my center informed me that some important movement of the enemy was going on in his front, beyond that of the line with which we were engaged. Mounting a large rock, I was able to see a considerable body of the enemy moving by the flank in rear of their line engaged, and passing from the direction of the foot of Great Round Top through the valley toward the front of my left. The close engagement not allowing any change of front, I immediately stretched my regiment to the left, by taking intervals by the left flank, and at the same time "refusing" my left wing, so that it was nearly at right angles with my right, thus occupying about twice the extent of

Joshua Lawrence Chamberlain.

our ordinary front, some of the companies being brought into single rank when the nature of the ground gave sufficient strength or shelter. My officers and men understood my wishes so well that this movement was executed under fire, the right wing keeping up fire, without giving the enemy any occasion to seize or even to suspect their advantage. But we were not a moment too soon; the enemy's flanking column having gained their desired direction, burst upon my left, where they evidently had expected an unguarded flank, with great demonstration.

We opened a brisk fire at close range, which was so sudden and effective that they soon fell back among the rocks and low trees in the valley, only to burst forth again with a shout, and rapidly advanced, firing as they came. They pushed up to within a dozen yards of us before the terrible effectiveness of our fire compelled them to break and take shelter.

They renewed the assault on our whole front, and for an hour the fighting was severe. Squads of the enemy broke through our line in several places, and the fight was literally hand to hand. The edge of the fight rolled backward and forward like a wave. The dead and wounded were now in our front and then in our rear. Forced from our position, we desperately recovered it, and pushed the enemy down to the foot of the slope. The intervals of the struggle were seized to remove our wounded (and those of the enemy also), to gather ammunition from the cartridge-boxes of disabled friend or foe on the field, and even to secure better muskets than the Enfields, which we found did not stand service well. Rude shelters were thrown up of the loose rocks that covered the ground.

Captain Woodward, commanding the Eighty-third Pennsylvania Volunteers, on my right, gallantly maintaining his fight, judiciously and with hearty co-operation made his movements conform to my necessities, so that my right was at no time exposed to a flank attack.

The enemy seemed to have gathered all their energies for their final assault. We had gotten our thin line into as good a shape as possible, when a strong force emerged from the scrub wood in the valley, as well as I could judge, in two lines in echelon by the right, and, opening a heavy fire, the first line came on as if they meant to sweep everything before them. We opened on them as well as we could with our scanty ammunition snatched from the field.

It did not seem possible to withstand another shock like this now coming on. Our loss had been severe. One-half of my left wing had fallen, and a third of my regiment lay just behind us, dead or badly wounded. At this moment my anxiety was increased by a great roar of musketry in my rear, on the farther or northerly slope of Little Round Top, apparently on the flank of the regular brigade, which was in support of Hazlett's battery on the crest behind us. The bullets from this attack struck into my left rear, and I feared that the enemy might have nearly surrounded the Little Round Top, and only a desperate chance was left for us. My ammunition was soon exhausted. My men were firing their last shot and getting ready to club their muskets.

It was imperative to strike before we were struck by this overwhelming force in a hand-to-hand fight, which we could not probably have withstood or survived. At that crisis, I ordered the bayonet. The word was enough. It ran like fire along the line, from man to man, and rose into a shout, with which they sprang forward upon the enemy, now not 30 yards away. The effect was surprising; many of the enemy's first line threw down their arms and surrendered. An officer fired his pistol at my head with one hand, while he handed me his sword with the other. Holding fast by our right, and swinging forward our left, we made an extended right wheel, before which the enemy's second line broke and fell back, fighting from tree to tree, many being captured, until we had swept the valley and cleared the front of nearly our entire brigade.

Meantime Captain Morrill with his skirmishers sent out from my left flank, with some dozen or fifteen of the U.S. Sharpshooters who had put themselves under his direction, fell upon the enemy as they were breaking, and by his demonstrations, as well as his well-directed fire, added much to the effect of the charge.

Having thus cleared the valley and driven the enemy up the western slope of the Great Round Top, not wishing to press so far out as to hazard the ground I was to hold by leaving it exposed to a sudden rush of the enemy, I succeeded (although with some effort to stop my men, who declared they were "on the road to Richmond") in getting the regiment into good order and resuming our original position.

Four hundred prisoners, including two field and several line officers, were sent to the rear. These were mainly from the Fifteenth and Forty-seventh Alabama Regiments, with some of the Fourth and Fifth Texas. One hundred and fifty of the enemy were found killed and wounded in our front.

★ ★ ★

Sunset from Little Round Top.

As the shadows lengthened toward evening on July 2, Chamberlain found himself responsible for preventing the enemy from rolling up the Union left. His orders from Vincent were to "hold that ground at all hazards." Chamberlain soon found out what that meant. For more than an hour, repeated assaults on Vincent's brigade (eventually reinforced by another brigade) surged back and forth, constantly increasing the pressure on the left flank held by the Twentieth Maine. Chamberlain and his senior captain, Ellis Spear (one of Chamberlain's former students at Bowdoin), extended and bent back their line in an attempt to prevent this disaster. Meanwhile, off to Chamberlain's right, on the west face of Little Round Top, the battle raged fiercely as Alabama and Texas regiments advanced from boulder to boulder up the hill. Vincent was mortally wounded, a colonel and the general commanding the reinforcing brigade were killed, and the commander of an artillery battery that had struggled into position was also killed.

A photograph of the Twentieth Maine memorial dedication;
Chamberlain is seated to the left of the furled flag.

Chamberlain seemed likely to meet the same fate. He had already been slightly wounded twice. With a third of his four hundred men down and the rest of them nearly out of ammunition, with the enemy apparently forming for yet another assault, the Twentieth Maine seemed finished. As Chamberlain later wrote, at this crisis "my thought was running deep. . . . Five minutes more of such a defensive, and the last roll-call would sound for us. Desperate as the chances were, there was nothing for it but to take the offensive. I stepped to the colors. The men turned toward me. One word was enough,—'BAYONET!' It caught like fire, and swept along the ranks." With a wild yell, the survivors of this two-hour firefight, led by their multilingual fighting professor, lurched downhill in a bayonet charge against the shocked Alabamians. The Twentieth drove them across the front of the next Union regiments in line, the Eighty-third Pennsylvania and the Forty-fourth New York, and together these three regiments captured more than two hundred of them (Chamberlain claimed almost four hundred).

The bust of Colonel Patrick O'Rorke.

The hero-worship of Chamberlain has prompted a minor backlash among some historians and park rangers who have grown tired of exaggerated questions and claims by visitors who want to see where Chamberlain performed these exploits. The revisionists claim that the men of the Twentieth spontaneously charged, or that Ellis Spear deserves the credit for the bayonet assault (though no one denies that it was Chamberlain who gave the order to fix bayonets). They quote the report of Colonel William C. Oates, commander of the Fifteenth Alabama (who, like Chamberlain, later became governor of his state), that he was in fact preparing to withdraw when the Twentieth Maine came screaming down the hill, and that the withdrawal was a retreat, not a rout. Oates doth protest too much. But there is no doubt that the Alabamians were exhausted and dehydrated after seemingly endless uphill fighting following a twenty-five-mile march to the battlefield.

It seems clear, however, that Chamberlain deserved the Congressional Medal of Honor he won for the defense of Little Round Top. He went on to become one of the war's most extraordinary soldiers. He rose to brigade command and, on June 18, 1864, was shot through the pelvis while leading his brigade in an assault at Petersburg. Such wounds were almost always fatal; Ulysses S. Grant promoted the supposedly dying colonel to brigadier general on the field—one of only two such occasions in the war. Chamberlain beat the odds and recovered to lead his brigade in the final campaign to Appomattox. At the battle of Quaker Road on March 29, 1865, he took another bullet, this one just below the heart, where it would have killed him had it not been deflected around his ribs by a leather case of field orders in his breast pocket. Chamberlain suffered two cracked ribs and a bruised arm, but continued to lead his brigade in several more fights during the next eleven days until the surrender at Appomattox. So impressed was Grant with his fighting professor that he selected Chamberlain to take charge of the Army of Northern Virginia's formal surrender at Appomattox.

In 1886, Chamberlain and other veterans of the Twentieth Maine returned to Gettysburg to dedicate their monument on Little Round Top. As we stand at the same spot, listen to Chamberlain's words on that occasion: "In great deeds, something abides. On great fields something stays. Forms change and pass; bodies disappear, but spirits linger, to consecrate the ground for the vision-place of souls. And reverent men and women from afar, and generations that know us not and that we know not of, heart-drawn to see where and by whom great things were suffered and done for them . . ." Little wonder that my students could not hold back the tears when I read these words to them here in 1987.

O'Rorke fell dead with a bullet through his neck while leading his 140th New York in a counterattack that saved that flank of the Union position from collapse.

The Twentieth Maine was not the only Union regiment whose heroics helped to save the day at Gettysburg. We will walk back to the west face of Little Round Top to study the interpretive markers and a dozen monuments there. One of the latter is a bust of Colonel Patrick O'Rorke, who graduated at the top of his West Point Class of 1861, the same class in which George Armstrong Custer, now a brigadier general, had finished last. O'Rorke fell dead with a bullet through his neck while leading his 140th New York in a counterattack that saved that flank of the Union position from collapse. We can also stand on a granite boulder next to a bronze statue of General Warren looking to the southwest where he professed to have seen the glint of sunlight reflected from enemy rifles.

From there we will head down the north slope of Little Round Top and continue on Sedgwick Avenue for a half-mile, where it becomes Hancock Avenue at about the point where it also begins to rise gradually from a swale to the higher ground of Cemetery Ridge. On the right, soon after the road becomes Hancock Avenue, is another impressive bronze statue, of Father William Corby standing with his right arm raised in blessing. Father Corby

The Twentieth Maine charging down
the slope of Little Round Top.

CALVARY OFFICER CUSTER JOINS THE BATTLE

OFFICIAL REPORT BY GENERAL CUSTER

On July 2, at the battle of Hunterstown, one squadron, under command of Captain Duggan, was detailed to hold the road leading into the town from the right front of it. One platoon was deployed as skirmishers on the left of the road leading into town from the rear. This platoon was actively engaged and did good service. The regiment sustained no loss upon this day.

★ ★ ★

General Custer on the Peninsular Campaign in 1862, a year before Gettysburg.

The monument for Father William Corby.

was chaplain of the famed Irish Brigade of Major General Winfield Scott Hancock's Second Corps. These five regiments, composed mainly of Irish-American Catholics, were much depleted by their losses in battle the previous year but still full of fight.

As the Third Corps was being pushed back from the Rose farm and the Wheatfield, Meade ordered Hancock to send a division to their support. That division included the Irish Brigade. Before they marched away from this spot, Father Corby climbed onto the boulder where his statue stands, and blessed the troops. After doing so, he added ominously that "the Catholic church refuses Christian burial to the soldier who turns his back upon the foe or deserts his flag." He then pronounced the Latin words of absolution for those who would not come back. Men from other regiments standing nearby also bowed their heads and accepted absolution even though they were Protestants; after all, it couldn't hurt.

The Irish brigade went into action three-quarters of a mile southwest of where Father Corby stands; its position is marked by a monument on Ayres Avenue that includes a bronze relief of the brigade mascot, an Irish wolfhound. Father Corby is one of the few Civil War chaplains honored by a monument (erected in 1910 by veterans of the Irish Brigade); he is surely the only one commemorated by two monuments, the second at Notre Dame University, where he served as president for many years after the Civil War.

A quarter-mile north of Father Corby's statue, on the left side of Hancock Avenue, stands one of the most impressive and moving monuments on the battlefield. It depicts a soldier running forward atop a high pedestal. The monument commemorates the attack by eight companies (262 men) of the First Minnesota against an entire Alabama brigade of 1,500 men. The First Minnesota had been in service longer than almost any other regiment in the Army of the Potomac. It had fought in nearly all of the battles since First Bull Run in July 1861, suffering some 260 killed and wounded before Gettysburg. There it would nearly double that total.

Reinforcements were on the way, but they could not arrive for ten minutes.

As the sun was setting on July 2, the First Minnesota was in line supporting an artillery battery (six guns) near the spot where the monument stands. Fragments of retreating Third Corps units streamed toward the rear while out of the haze of gunsmoke appeared a line of Alabama troops emerging from a thicket three hundred yards away. All other Union infantry in this sector had gone to the Wheatfield earlier. In a few minutes the Alabama brigade would breach this crucial position unless it was stopped. Hancock galloped up and shouted, "My God! Are these all the men we have here?" Reinforcements were on the way, but they could not arrive for ten minutes. Hancock needed to buy that much time, even if it cost every man in the regiment. Turning to Colonel William Colvill, Hancock pointed to the Alabamians and yelled, "Advance, Colonel, and take those colors."

Without hesitation, the 262 men fixed bayonets and began double-timing forward. "Every man realized in an instant what that order meant—death or wounds to us all," wrote Colvill, who was wounded in the attack, "and every man saw and accepted the necessity for the sacrifice." With a yell they tore into the Alabamians and bought Hancock his ten minutes and more. The Confederates made it no farther. Seventy Minnesotans didn't make it at all, and another 145 were wounded or missing. This casualty rate of 82 percent of those engaged was the highest of the war for any Union regiment in a single action.

As the fighting died away at dark on the Union left, the volume of artillery and rifle fire a mile or two northeast at Culp's and East Cemetery Hills continued unabated. This part of the battlefield was the most visited by tourists in the 1870s and 1880s, for it was the first land purchased by the Gettysburg Battlefield Memorial Association, a private group formed in 1864 to preserve and commemorate the battlefield. Today, however, it is the least visited portion of the battlefield, partly because it is only on the "optional" route of the Park Service's self-guided auto tour, and partly because all of the action described in *The Killer Angels* and the film/miniseries *Gettysburg* occurred on other parts of the battlefield. But the Culp's Hill/East Cemetery Hill fighting was intense, and just as important to the battle's outcome as elsewhere. If the Confederates had captured this position or achieved a breakthrough, it would have been as

The First Minnesota monument with shamrock detail around the top of the pedastal.

This postcard promoting Spangler's Spring is from a line of Gettysburg postcards from the 1930s.

disastrous for the Union cause as the loss of Little Round Top or Cemetery Ridge.

From the First Minnesota monument we proceed north a tenth of a mile, turn right on Pleasonton Avenue, left onto the Taneytown Road (Route 134), and right at Hunt Avenue, following it for a half mile to a T-crossing at the Baltimore Pike (Route 97). We'll turn right there, then after three-tenths of a mile left onto Slocum Avenue, which will wind through the woods for a half-mile to the optional auto-tour stop at Spangler's Spring. The interpretive markers in this area describe the actions that took place on the evening of July 2 and the morning of July 3. The many monuments alongside the road as one proceeds up the steep grade to the observation tower commemorate the Union regiments that fought here. We will follow that route in a few moments, but first we pause to consider another long-standing Gettysburg myth.

We are advised not to drink the water from Spangler's Spring today. But no such advisory existed in 1863, when this unpolluted water was a godsend for thirsty soldiers. The lines of the opposing armies were close together near the spring on the night of July 2–3. As the theme of Blue-Gray reconciliation grew to powerful proportions from the 1880s onward, a story arose that on this dark night both Confederate and Union soldiers went to the spring to fill their canteens. There they encountered each other, called a truce, talked over the battle, and traded jokes before returning to their own lines. This story fit perfectly with the spirit of joint Blue-Gray veterans' reunions that began at Gettysburg as early as 1887.

For decades, battlefield guides and the Park Service's interpretive marker and literature told the romantic tale of fraternization at Spangler's Spring. But there is no truth to it, and to-day the guides and marker tell the real story. When a captain in the Forty-sixth Pennsylvania approached the spring with several empty canteens, he discovered enemy soldiers filling theirs. He backed away silently and returned to his own lines, thanking his lucky stars he had escaped capture. That is the fact, but it is far less interesting than the legend and did not fit the theme of North-South reconciliation, which explains why legend long prevailed over fact.

Confederates controlled the area around Spangler's Spring because five of the six brigades of the Union Twelfth Corps had gone to the left in response to calls for reinforcements against Longstreet's assault. (As it turned out, most of them were not needed.) They left behind only the five New York regiments of Brigadier General George S. Greene's brigade to hold the hill. This move opened a splendid opportunity for the Confederates. Lee's plan for July 2 had called for Ewell's corps to convert its demonstration against Culp's Hill into a real attack if and when Meade weakened his right to reinforce his left. Meade did so, but Ewell was slow to seize the opportunity. The attack against Culp's Hill by Major General Edward Johnson's division

The reconciliation myth of soldiers from both sides drinking from Spangler's Spring is perpetuated in the caption of this stereo card, which reads, "Spangler Spring, where boys in Blue and Gray drank together in pauses of the battle, Gettysburg."

and against Cemetery Hill by two brigades of Jubal Early's division did not get started until almost dusk.

Attacking up the steep east side of Culp's Hill from the valley of Rock Creek, Johnson's three brigades of seventeen regiments outnumbered Greene's New Yorkers by more than three to one. Greene contracted his lines to defend four hundred yards of trenches along the upper slope, abandoning the other four hundred yards leading down to Spangler's Spring. Traces of these trenches can be seen east of Slocum Avenue as we ascend the hill. The attackers over-ran the empty trenches. They then turned right to attack the Union line end-on. Holding this flank was the 137th New York, commanded by Colonel David Ireland, whose predicament here was the same as Colonel Chamberlain's at the other end of the Union line. Just as Chamberlain bent back his line to the left, Ireland bent his to the right. And the 137th fought just as courageously against superior numbers as the Twentieth Maine did—lacking only the bayonet charge. But no novelist has told the story of the 137th, and few visitors stop to view its monument on the right of Slocum Avenue about a hundred yards past the intersection with Geary Avenue. It is worth our while to stop and contemplate this monument before going on to the top of Culp's Hill and climbing the observation tower that rises next to the splendid bronze statue of General Greene, who remembered his successful defense of Culp's Hill until his death thirty-six years later at the age of ninety-eight.

ON THE SECOND DAY'S BATTLE

By Abner Doubleday

There has been much discussion and a good deal of crimination and recrimination among the rebel generals engaged as to which of them lost the battle of Gettysburg.

I have already alluded to the fact that universal experience demonstrates that columns converging on a central force almost invariably fail in their object and are beaten in detail. Gettysburg seems to me a striking exemplification of this; repeated columns of assault launched by Lee against our lines came up in succession and were

Johnson's attack on Culp's Hill.

defeated before the other parts of his army could arrive in time to sustain the attack. He realized the old fable. The peasant could not break the bundle of fagots, but he could break one at a time until all were gone.

Lee's concave form of battle was a great disadvantage, for it took him three times as long as it did us to communicate with different parts of his line, and concentrate troops. His couriers who carried orders and the reinforcements he sent moved on the circumference and ours on the chord of the arc.

The two armies were about a mile apart. The Confederates—Longstreet and Hill—occupied Seminary Ridge, which runs parallel to Cemetery Ridge, upon which our forces were posted. Ewell's corps, on the rebel left, held the town, Hill the centre, and Longstreet the right.

Lee could easily have manoeuvred Meade out of his strong position on the heights, and should have done so. When he determined to attack, he should have commenced at daybreak, for all his force was up except Pickett's division; while two corps of the Union army, the Fifth and Sixth, were still far away, and two brigades of the Third Corps were also absent.

Major General Edward Johnson.

Looking northwest from the tower, we see open fields in the near foreground. At dusk on July 2, two brigades of Jubal Early's division swept across this swale between Culp's Hill and East Cemetery Hill to attack the remnants of their Eleventh Corps adversaries of the previous day. Descending from the tower, we will follow Slocum Avenue until it turns left; instead of turning where the auto-tour sign beckons us, we will continue straight ahead on Wainwright Avenue. This narrow road marks the position held by two brigades of the Eleventh Corps. Once again these hapless regiments broke, streaming back up the steep hill to our left. On came the Confederates, threatening to capture the Union artillery at the top. We too will hike up this hill to look at the gun emplacements. Timely Union reinforcements coming from the area that is now the National Cemetery counterattacked and drove Early's brigades down the hill and back to their starting point. Much of this fighting was hand-to-hand and took place after dark, when soldiers were in almost as much danger from friendly fire as from the enemy.

Both armies settled down to an uneasy night interrupted by frequent firing from pickets alarmed by shadows and noises. Each side had suffered almost ten thousand casualties in what turned out to be perhaps the second bloodiest day of the war (the one-day battle of Antietam, with a combined total of 23,000 casualties, was the bloodiest). Confederates had made some gains at great cost, but had failed to achieve a breakthrough. Southern attacks had lacked coordination. Lee had followed his customary practice of issuing general orders but letting his corps commanders execute them as they thought best. The usual skills of generalship in the Army of Northern Virginia seem to have gone missing this day, especially on Ewell's front against Culp's and Cemetery Hills. On the Union side, by contrast, officers from Meade down to regimental colonels acted with initiative and coolness. They moved reinforcements to the right spots and counterattacked at the right times.

The 137th New York monument on Culp's Hill.

Ewell's corps' attack on Cemetery Hill.

ON LEE AND JEB STUART

By Abner Doubleday

It seems strange that Lee should suppose that the Union army would continue inactive all this time, south of Washington, where it was only confronted by Stuart's cavalry, and it is remarkable to find him so totally in the dark with regard to Hooker's movements. It has been extensively assumed by rebel writers that this ignorance was caused by the injudicious raid made by Stuart, who thought it would be a great benefit to the Confederate cause if he could ride entirely around the Union lines and rejoin Lee's advance at York. He had made several of these circuits during his military career, and had gained important advantages from them in way of breaking up communications, capturing despatches, etc. It is thought that he hoped by threatening Hooker's rear to detain him and delay his crossing the river, and thus give time to Lee to capture Harrisburg, and perhaps Philadelphia. His raid on this occasion was undoubtedly a mistake. When he rejoined the main body, his men were exhausted, his horses broken down, and the battle of Gettysburg was nearly over. As cavalry are the eyes of an army, it has been said that Stuart's absence prevented Lee from ascertaining the movements and position of Hooker's army. Stuart has been loudly blamed by the rebel chroniclers for leaving the main body, but this is unjust; Lee not only knew of the movement, but approved it; for he directed Stuart to pass between Hooker and Washington, and move with part of his force to Carlisle and the other part to Gettysburg. Besides, Stuart left Robertson's and Jones' brigades behind, with orders to follow up the rear of the Union army until it crossed, and then to rejoin the main body. In the meantime they were to hold the gaps in the Blue Ridge, for fear Hooker might send a force to occupy them. These two brigades, with Imboden's brigade, and White's battalion, made quite a large cavalry force: Imboden, however, was also detached to break up the Baltimore and Ohio Railroad to prevent forces from the West from taking Lee in rear; all of which goes to show how sensitive the Confederate commander was in regard to any danger threatening his communications with Richmond.

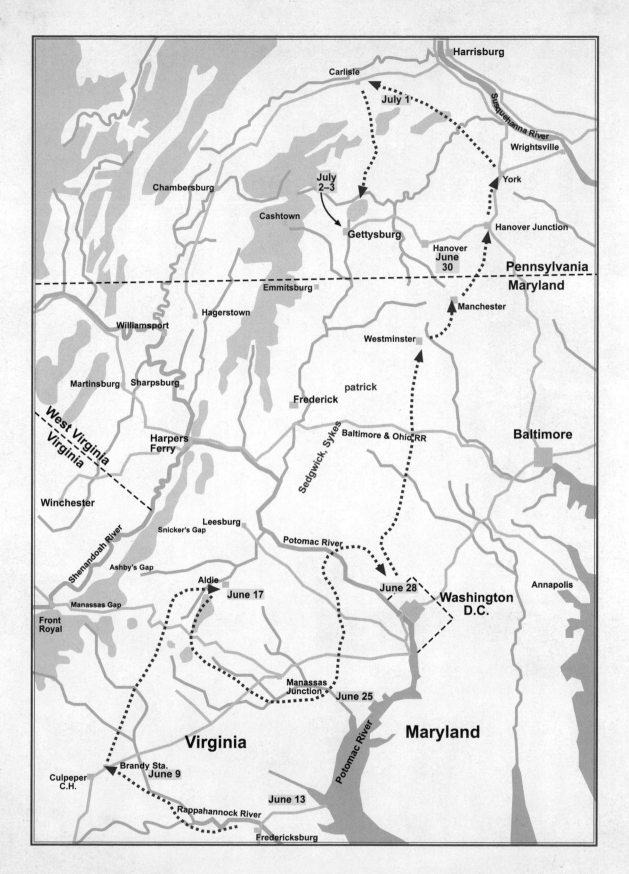

Stuart's long ride leading to Gettysburg.

A chromolithograph of Lee.

Despite the stout Yankee resistance, Lee believed that his indomitable veterans had won the day. One more push, he thought, and the enemy would break. Pickett's division and Stuart's three cavalry brigades had finally arrived and would be available on the morrow. (Across the way, Union Major General John Sedgwick's Sixth Corps had also arrived, more than balancing the Confederate reinforcements.) Lee's mood and physical condition at Gettysburg have been the subjects of some controversy. He seemed unusually excited by the supposed successes of these two days. At the same time he may have been weakened by a touch of diarrhea. Or perhaps, as the novelist Michael Shaara suggested in *The Killer Angels*, a flare-up of Lee's heart condition left him by turns belligerent and indecisive, gnawed by the conviction that he had little time left.

Historians have tended to discount Shaara's interpretation. But two surgeons at the University of Virginia medical school, who also happen to be Civil War buffs, have offered evidence to support it. In March 1863 Lee suffered what was probably a myocardial infarction. By his own account, Lee did not feel he had fully recovered and reported himself "more and more incapable of exertion." Piecing together Lee's own references to his health and those of his physician, these two surgeons suggest that Lee had ischemic heart disease—an inadequate supply of blood to the heart—which eventually killed him in 1870 at the age of sixty-three. "This illness," the doctors concluded in a medical journal article, may have "had a major influence on the battle of Gettysburg."

Precisely what influence is not clear. Did illness cloud Lee's judgment? Perhaps. But what we might call the "Chancellorsville Syndrome" may have been more important than Lee's health in this regard. Lee continued to think that he could win at Gettysburg as he had won two months earlier against greater numerical odds—by attacking. He had hit the Union flank at Chancellorsville and followed it up with a frontal assault, which had worked. He intended to try similar tactics at Gettysburg. He had come to Pennsylvania in quest of a decisive victory; he was determined not to leave without trying to achieve it. He believed that Meade had weakened his center to reinforce the flanks that were attacked on July 2. With Pickett's fresh division as a spearhead, he would send three divisions against the enemy center. He would also have Stuart's cavalry circle around and come in on the Union rear, while Ewell would again assail the Union right to clamp the pincers when Pickett broke through the front. With proper coordination and leadership, his invincible troops could not fail.

ON MEADE AT THE END OF THE SECOND DAY

By Abner Doubleday

At night a council of war was held, in which it was unanimously voted to stay and fight it out. Meade was displeased with the result, and although he acquiesced in the decision, he said angrily, "Have it your own way, gentlemen, but Gettysburg is no place to fight a battle in." The fact that a portion of the enemy actually prolonged our line on the right and that our centre had been pierced during the day, made him feel far from confident. He thought it better to retreat with what he had, than run the risk of losing all.

Meade's night council.

This colorized print of a black-and-white negative, known as a photochrom, shows Meade's headquarters.

The Confederates would continue attacking against the Union's tactically superior position.

Over on the Union side of the lines, Northern officers pondered the day's events and wondered what would come on the morrow. Meade called a meeting of his corps commanders in the small farmhouse that served as his headquarters. (The house is still there, about three hundred yards east of the equestrian monument to Meade just behind the scene of the next day's fighting at the climax of Pickett's Charge.) Meade asked for a vote by his generals on whether to retreat or to stay and fight. They all voted to stay.

A myth long persisted that Meade wanted to retreat, but was only persuaded to the contrary by this vote. The origins of the myth lay with two Daniels: Dan Sickles and Major General Daniel Butterfield, Meade's chief of staff, whose main claim to fame was his composition, the previous year, of the bugle call "Taps." Both Daniels were cronies of the deposed army commander Joe Hooker, and their loyalties lay more with Hooker than with his successor. When Meade took over the army on June 28, there was not time to replace the experienced Butterfield with a new chief of staff before the battle was upon him. Butterfield later claimed that on July 2 Meade had instructed him to prepare orders for a retreat. What actually happened was that Meade asked Butterfield to draw a map of all the roads in the Union rear and to prepare contingency plans for a withdrawal in case it became necessary. This was only prudent, and Meade could be justly criticized if he had failed to prepare for every contingency.

But Meade, like his corps commanders, wanted to stay and fight. Butterfield's motive for stating the contrary was probably a desire to discredit Meade in order to make Hooker look better. As for Sickles, while recovering from the loss of his leg he smarted at criticism of his move forward to the Peach Orchard contrary to orders. He continued to believe that this move had saved the army and won the battle—and also that by precipitating the fighting on July 2, it had undercut Meade's intention to retreat.

MEADE'S REPORT TO MAJOR GENERAL HALLECK AT THE END OF THE SECOND DAY

HEADQUARTERS ARMY OF THE POTOMAC, JULY 2, 1863, 11 PM

The enemy attacked me about 4 PM this day, and after one of the severest contests of the war, was repulsed at all points. We have suffered considerably in killed and wounded; among the former are Brigadier General Paul Zook, and among the wounded, Generals Sickles, Barlow, Graham, and Warren slightly. We have taken a large number of prisoners. I shall remain in my present position to-morrow, but am not prepared to say, until better advised of the condition of the army, whether my operations will be of an offensive or defensive character.

Meade and his staff. Meade is seated right, front.

Sickles lived long enough to argue this case many times. Elected to Congress in 1892, he introduced the bill that created Gettysburg National Military Park in 1895. He made sure that the park boundaries included the area where his Third Corps had fought, so that visitors would always be able to see why he took them forward to the higher ground at the Peach Orchard and along the Emmitsburg Road. In 1897, after persistent lobbying, the army belatedly awarded Sickles the Congressional Medal of Honor for gallantry at Gettysburg. In his ninety-fourth year, Sickles attended the huge fiftieth anniversary commemoration of the battle at Gettysburg, still insisting that his move had set the stage for victory. Sickles died the following year, having outlived every other corps commander at Gettysburg.

Having decided to stay and fight, Meade made his preparations for the morrow. Two divisions of Hancock's tough Second Corps held the Union center just forward of Meade's headquarters. One of those divisions was commanded by General John Gibbon, a native of North Carolina who had remained loyal to the flag under which he had served for twenty years while three of his brothers went with the Confederacy. Looking back years after the battle, Gibbon recalled that Meade told him on that night of July 2 that "if Lee attacks tomorrow, it will be in your front," because he had tried both flanks and failed. Gibbon gritted his teeth and told Meade that he would be ready if Lee came his way.

This antique, and slightly weathered, photograph shows cheering for Sickles, who is seated in front, at the 1913 Gettysburg reunion.

DAY THREE

July 3, 1863

JULY 3 dawned warm and humid—normal for midsummer in Gettysburg. As the light strengthened, firing broke out and grew louder on the Culp's Hill lines, where it had died away only seven hours earlier. The Union Twelfth Corps brigades that had departed to reinforce the left had returned during the night and were determined to regain their lost trenches in the morning. We return now to the Spangler's Spring area to discuss what happened there on that morning of July 3. Ewell had also reinforced the Confederate units at Culp's Hill, doubling their numbers overnight. Both sides planned to attack there at first light—the Federals to regain the trenches they had abandoned, the Confederates to renew their effort to capture the hill. The Yankees struck first, at 4:30 AM, with an artillery barrage against the Confederates in those captured trenches on the southern slope of the hill. Soon after, Confederate infantry renewed their attack on the higher slopes where the fighting had taken place the previous evening.

*Behind the breastworks on Culp's Hill during
the morning battle of July 3rd.*

The Second Massachusetts monument.

Once again the 137th New York found itself in the thick of the action, but this time it had plenty of help. Back and forth for several hours on this line came attacks and counterattacks, in the woods and in a small clearing called Pardee Field. Some fifty monuments and markers crowded into the half-mile from Spangler's Spring up to the observation tower testify to the intensity of fighting for nearly seven hours on this hot morning. Most of the time it was the Confederates who attacked, but each time they were driven back.

One dramatic Union assault in late morning by the Second Massachusetts and Twenty-seventh Indiana against the Confederate left was also repulsed with heavy loss, a story told by the interpretive marker and the monuments of these two regiments near Spangler's Spring. Both were elite regiments; most of the Second Massachusetts's officers were Harvard alumni. In a few minutes, about 250 men in the two regiments were shot down, ninety-five of them fatally.

Another poignant event took place on this flank that morning. Twenty-two-year-old Wesley Culp was a private in the Second Virginia Infantry, which took position as skirmishers on the Confederate left across Rock Creek, about four hundred yards east of Spangler's Spring. Culp had grown up in Gettysburg where, like Henry Wentz, he had learned the trade of carriage-maker. Also like Wentz, he had gone to Virginia before the war, when his employer moved the carriage-making business to Shepherdstown. Young Culp had

Opposite: Woods on Culp's hill, riddled by musket fire.

Mary "Jenny" Virginia Wade was killed in her sister's kitchen by a stray bullet.

joined the local militia there, which became Company B of the Second Virginia when the war broke out. Now he was back at Gettysburg, fighting near the hill named after his great-grandfather, who had established a farm near the hill now owned by Wesley's cousin Henry Culp. As a boy, Wesley had splashed in the local swimming hole in Rock Creek; now as a soldier he was taking potshots at Yankees along the creek; one of them took a shot at him and the bullet went home. No monument marks the spot where Wesley Culp was killed; no one recorded where he was buried; it may have been in land owned by his cousin.

Wesley Culp was not the only native of Gettysburg killed on July 3. In the town itself, Confederates had barricaded Baltimore Street three blocks south of the square. From there and from houses nearby, sharpshooters traded shots with Union skirmishers on Cemetery Hill. Most residents of Gettysburg hid in their cellars to get out of the line of fire. One who did not was Mary Virginia Wade, known as Jenny, a comely twenty-year-old lass who was at her sister's house on Baltimore Street that day to help take care of her sister's newborn baby. Jenny Wade was engaged to Corporal Johnston Skelly of the Eighty-seventh Pennsylvania, which she knew was somewhere in Virginia. She too wanted to do her part for the war effort, so, despite warnings, she went to the kitchen that morning to bake biscuits for Union skirmishers. Suddenly a bullet from a Confederate rifle smashed through two doors and lodged in Jenny's back. She died not knowing that a few days earlier her fiancé had also died of a wound he received in the battle of Winchester on June 15—a battle in which Wesley Culp had fought as his regiment was moving north toward Pennsylvania. Jenny Wade was the only civilian death in the battle of Gettysburg. The house where she was killed is still there to be visited, immediately south of the Holiday Inn.

The exchange of sniper fire between rebels in Gettysburg and Yankees behind stone walls on Cemetery Hill never ceased during daylight hours. But on Culp's Hill the firing died away about 11:00 AM. The Confederates pulled back to count their killed and wounded, which were at least double those of the two Union divisions defending the hill. If the Army of Northern Virginia was to win the battle of Gettysburg, it would not do so at Culp's Hill. One part of Lee's three-pronged effort on July 3 had failed. The second part was about to begin.

East Cavalry Field.

Early that morning, Jeb Stuart rode east from Gettysburg at the head of six thousand Confederate cavalry. He intended to circle south about three miles east of Gettysburg, and then turn west to come in on the Union rear along Cemetery Ridge. We will follow the route of Stuart's troopers to what is today called East Cavalry Field. Returning from Culp's Hill to Baltimore Street, we turn north to the traffic circle in downtown Gettysburg, then turn right on York Street (US Route 30) and proceed almost three miles to a right turn onto Cavalry Field Road. Another mile brings us to a sharp right along a ridgeline (Confederate Cavalry Avenue) from which we gaze southward over open, rolling farmland with the historic Rummel farm in the near distance. At about 1:00 PM the Confederate horsemen advanced south along this ridge, dismounted skirmishers leading the way. So far they had spotted no enemy. The way to the Union rear seemed open.

They soon encountered plenty of Yankees, however, about five thousand of them in three brigades. One was a Michigan brigade commanded by Brigadier General George Armstrong Custer, who had been jumped several grades to that rank only four days earlier. Having graduated last in his West Point class, Custer had proven in the war's first two years that there was no necessary correlation between class rank and fighting ability. Custer is remembered today mainly for his foolhardy decision at the Little Bighorn in 1876 that led to his death and that of all the men with him. But he should be remembered also for his successful hell-for-leather record as a cavalry commander during the last two years of the Civil War, starting on this hot afternoon at Gettysburg.

When this photo was taken in 1865, Custer was a Major General.

For two hours—the same two hours of the artillery duel and the beginning of the Pickett-Pettigrew assault back at Gettysburg—fast and furious cavalry attacks and counterattacks, mounted and dismounted, surged back and forth across these fields. At one point in the seesawing firefight, with Union horsemen hard pressed and falling back, Custer rode to the head of one of his regiments, the Seventh Michigan, and with a shout of "Come on, you Wolverines," led them at the gallop in a Hollywood-style charge that blunted the rebel advance. Counterattacked in turn, the bloodied Wolverines tumbled back in disorder.

We'll follow Confederate Cavalry Avenue south, to where it bends sharply left and becomes Gregg Avenue. Another half-mile brings us to a roadside marker and the impressive Michigan monument, a hundred yards south of the road. A confused melee in the fields south of this monument resolved itself into a renewed offensive led by the South Carolina brigade of Brigadier General Wade Hampton, a skilled commander and reputedly the South's richest planter. Custer

The Michigan Cavalry Monument.

once again led a mounted charge, this time by the First Michigan. As the South Carolinians and Wolverines thundered toward each other, an awed Pennsylvania trooper looking on described what happened next: "As the two columns approached each other, the pace of each increased, when suddenly a crash, like the falling of timber, betokened the crisis. So sudden and violent was the collision that many of the horses were turned end over end and crushed their riders beneath them. The clashing of sabers, the firing of pistols, and demands for surrender, and cries of combatants, filled the air."

Custer's horse went down, but he jumped up and mounted a riderless horse and continued to slash away with his saber, scarcely missing a beat. Other Northern units closed in on Hampton's flanks; one New Jersey trooper charged through the confusion and sent Hampton to the rear with severe saber wounds to his head. Their leader down, and beset by angry Yankees yelling like maniacs, the rebel horsemen retreated to the protection of their artillery on the ridge from which they had started. Not long after Pickett's Virginians reeled back from Seminary Ridge, three miles to the west, Stuart recoiled from what has been known ever since as East Cavalry Field.

About the time the cavalry action began, the temporary calm back in Gettysburg was shattered by two cannon shots from Seminary Ridge at 1:07 PM. This was the signal for 150 Confederate guns to soften up the point of attack near a copse of woods on Cemetery Ridge that Lee had selected for the target of his infantry assault. Union guns replied, and for almost two hours the rapid fire of more than 250 cannons shook the countryside. Owing to some freak acoustic condition of the atmosphere, several people in the Pittsburgh area, 150 miles to the west, heard this artillery barrage, while residents of Chambersburg, only twenty-five miles away, heard little or nothing.

After the first few minutes, the Confederate shells began to go too far before exploding, causing havoc a couple of hundred yards in the rear of the Union lines, but leaving infantry and artillery at the front relatively unscathed. Confederate gunners failed to realize the inaccuracy of their fire because the smoke from all these guns hung in the calm, humid air and obscured their view. Several explanations for this Confederate overshooting have been offered. One theory is that as the gun barrels heated up, the powder exploded with greater force. Another is that the recoil scarred the ground, lowering the carriage trails and elevating the barrels ever so slightly. The most ingenious explanation grows out of an explosion at the Richmond arsenal in March that took it out of production for several weeks. The Army of Northern Virginia had to depend on arsenals farther south for production of many of the shells for the invasion of Pennsylvania. Confederate gunners did not realize that fuses on these shells burned more slowly than those from the Richmond arsenal; thus the shells whose fuses they tried to time for explosion above front-line Union troops, showering them with lethal shrapnel, exploded a split second too late, after the shells had passed over.

Whatever the reason, the Confederate artillery barrage did not accomplish its purpose. Nevertheless, after an hour or so, the Union chief of artillery, Brigadier General Henry J. Hunt, began to withdraw some batteries from action as a ruse to convince the Confederates that they had been knocked out and also to save ammunition for the infantry attack he knew was coming.

Confederate cannon fire.

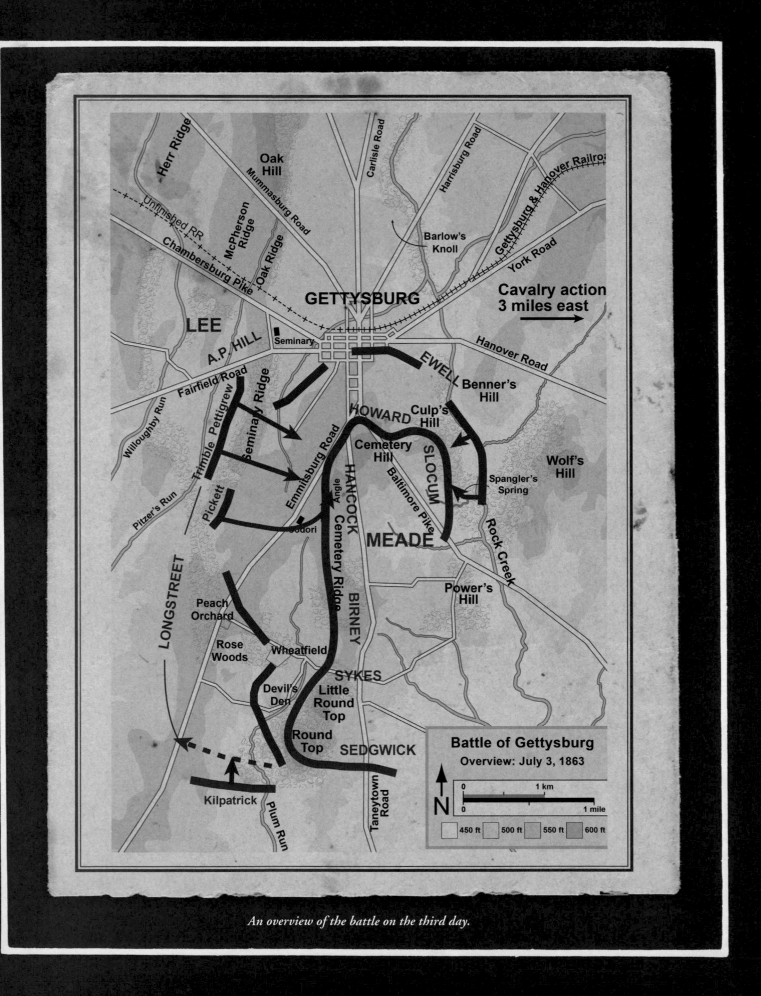

An overview of the battle on the third day.

*General Lee mounted on Traveller atop the Virginia monument. For
a detail image of the base of the monument, see page 84.*

Our next stop is the jump-off point for that attack. To get there from East Cavalry Field, we return to town on the Hanover Road (State Route 116), and continue west from down-town Gettysburg on Middle Street, which becomes the Fairfield Road (still Route 116). At the top of Seminary Ridge, we will turn left at the stoplight onto West Confederate Avenue, which follows the Confederate line south. The numerous cannons on our left, pointing at Cemetery Ridge across the fields, mark the positions of some of those Confederate guns firing fast and furiously that hot afternoon of July 3.

A little more than a mile after our turn, we will pull into the parking area at the Virginia monument. After viewing this impressive sculpture portraying in bronze several representative Confederate soldiers at the base, with Robert E. Lee far above, mounted on his favorite horse, Traveller, we will walk a hundred yards east to the edge of the woods on the right. From this point the Confederate artillery stretched still another three-quarters of a mile south, all firing at the Union lines. The copse of trees visible across the fields was their central aiming point.

CUSTER'S MEN FIGHT OFF CONFEDERATES

REPORT BY BRIGADIER GENERAL GEORGE ARMSTRONG CUSTER

On July 3, engagement 2 or 3 miles to the right of the Two Taverns, in which this regiment charged in close column upon Hampton's brigade, using the saber only, and driving the enemy from the field, with a loss to this regiment of 6 officers and 80 men.

Custer fought with his sword in the close combat at Gettysburg.

These fields were crisscrossed in 1863 by Virginia worm fences or post-and-rail fences enclosing small fields of grain, corn, and hay. Farmers in southern Pennsylvania customarily fenced in their crops and left livestock free to graze in open pastures and woods. These fences formed an obstacle to infantry moving across the fields. The Park Service intends to rebuild replica fences where they existed in 1863. But to be entirely realistic, many of the fence rails should then be thrown down, for by the afternoon of July 3, 1863, soldiers of both armies had already done precisely that during the previous two days. And when the Confederate infantry attacked across these fields, details of soldiers ran ahead of the main body to pull down many of the remaining rails.

That morning Lee and Longstreet had again disagreed about tactical plans for the day. Longstreet had informed Lee shortly after dawn, "General, I have had my scouts out all night, and I find that you still have an excellent chance to move around to the left of Meade's army and maneuver him into attacking us." But Lee was no more in the mood for such a move than he had been twenty-four hours earlier. "The enemy is there," he said, pointing toward the Union line, and "I am going to take them where they are." He ordered Longstreet to prepare Pickett's fresh division and most of the brigades in Hill's two divisions that had fought on July 1—about twelve thousand men altogether—for an assault on the Union center near that copse of trees. They would be supported by other brigades from Major General Richard Anderson's division of Hill's corps.

Post-and-rail fences on the battlefield with worm fences in the distance.

ON LEE AND THE BATTLE PLANS FOR THE THIRD DAY

By James Longstreet

He did not give or send me orders for the morning of the third day, nor did he reinforce me by Pickett's brigades for morning attack. As his head-quarters were about four miles from the command, I did not ride over, but sent, to report the work of the second day. In the absence of orders, I had scouting parties out during the night in search of a way by which we might strike the enemy's left, and push it down towards his centre. I found a way that gave some promise of results, and was about to move the command, when he rode over after sunrise and gave his orders. His plan was to assault the enemy's left centre by a column to be composed of McLaws's and Hood's divisions reinforced by Pickett's brigades. I thought that it would not do; that the point had been fully tested the day before, by more men, when all were fresh; that the enemy was there looking for us, as we heard him during the night putting up his defences; that the divisions of McLaws and Hood were holding a mile along the right of my line against twenty thousand men, who would follow their withdrawal, strike the flank of the assaulting column, crush it, and get on our rear towards the Potomac River; that thirty thousand men was the minimum of force necessary for the work; that even such force would need close co-operation on other parts of the line; that the column as he proposed to organize it would have only about thirteen thousand men (the divisions having lost a third of their numbers the day before); that the column would have to march a mile under concentrating battery fire, and a thousand yards under long-range musketry; that the conditions were different from those in the days of Napoleon, when field batteries had a range of six hundred yards and musketry about sixty yards.

He said the distance was not more than fourteen hundred yards. General Meade's estimate was a mile or a mile and a half (Captain Long, the guide of the field of Gettysburg in 1888, stated that it was a trifle over a mile). He then concluded that the divisions of McLaws and Hood could remain on the defensive line; that he would reinforce by divisions of the Third Corps and Pickett's brigades, and stated the point

At camp.

to which the march should be directed. I asked the strength of the column. He stated fifteen thousand. Opinion was then expressed that the fifteen thousand men who could make successful assault over that field had never been arrayed for battle; but he was impatient of listening, and tired of talking, and nothing was left but to proceed. General Alexander was ordered to arrange the batteries of the front of the First and Third Corps, those of the Second were supposed to be in position; Colonel Walton was ordered to see that the batteries of the First were supplied with ammunition, and to prepare to give the signal-guns for the opening combat. The infantry of the Third Corps to be assigned were Heth's and Pettigrew's divisions and Wilcox's brigade.

Major General George E. Pickett.

The attackers would have to advance across these open fields in front of us, under artillery fire almost every step of the way. When they got across the stout post-and-rail fences lining the Emmitsburg Road (most of which had not been pulled down), they would come under rifle fire from Union infantry sheltered by stone walls, fences, and shallow trenches. "General Lee," Longstreet later reported himself to have said, "I have been a soldier all my life. I have been with soldiers engaged in fights by couples, by squads, companies, regiments, divisions, and armies, and should know as well as anyone what soldiers can do. It is my opinion that no fifteen thousand men ever arrayed for battle can take that position."

Irritated by this near-insubordination, Lee replied impatiently that his army had over-come similar odds before—the implication being that Longstreet had not been present at Chancellorsville and therefore did not know what he was talking about—and they could do it again. Longstreet was his senior corps commander, and Lee wanted him to organize the attack despite his reluctance. "My heart was heavy," Longstreet recalled. "I could see the desperate and hopeless nature of the charge and the cruel slaughter it would cause. That day at Gettysburg was the saddest of my life."

Brigadier Generals Lewis A. Armistead and Richard B. Garnett.

Longstreet's account may have been colored by hindsight. On the other hand, Confederate officers noted his heavy countenance as he organized the artillery for bombardment and the infantry for attack. He would have six brigades in addition to Pickett's three in the primary attack, and at least two more in support. Except for Pickett's division, these troops would not come from his own corps, which had been too badly shot up the previous day to be ready to fight again. Instead, the other six brigades in the primary attack would come from Henry Heth's and Dorsey Pender's divisions of A. P. Hill's corps. They had been badly mangled on July 1, but at least the survivors had had a day of rest. They would not be under their usual commanders, however; Heth had been wounded on the first day and Pender on the second (Pender would die of his wound two weeks later). Brigadier Generals J. Johnston Pettigrew and Isaac Trimble took their places. Four of the six brigades in these two divisions were also under new commanders this day—all of them colonels—which did not augur well for the steadiness of these units if they ran into heavy resistance.

Major General George E. Pickett's all-Virginia division would constitute nearly half of the attacking force. They waited with nervous impatience to go in and get it over with. Like Custer, Pickett had graduated last in his West Point class (of 1846). And like Custer, he wore his long hair in ringlets. With his face adorned by a drooping mustache and goatee, Pickett looked like a cross between a Cavalier dandy and a riverboat gambler. He affected the style of Sir Walter Scott. His division had been involved only in skirmishes since the battle of Antietam, more than nine months earlier, and Pickett himself had seen little action since he was wounded in the Seven Days battles a year before. He was eager to win everlasting glory at Gettysburg.

ARTILLERY FIRE ON THE THIRD DAY

By James Longstreet

$\mathcal{A}$ note to Alexander directed that Pickett should not be called until the artillery practice indicated fair opportunity. Then I rode to a woodland hard by, to lie down and study for some new thought that might aid the assaulting column. In a few minutes report came from Alexander that he would only be able to judge of the effect of his fire by the return of that of the enemy, as his infantry was not exposed to view, and the smoke of the batteries would soon cover the field. He asked, if there

A cannon at Gettysburg.

Confederate reenactors in a haze of smoke common to battlefields.

was an alternative, that it be carefully considered before the batteries opened, as there was not enough artillery ammunition for this and another trial if this should not prove favorable.

He was informed that there was no alternative; that I could find no way out of it; that General Lee had considered and would listen to nothing else; that orders had gone for the guns to give signal for the batteries; that he should call the troops at the first opportunity or lull in the enemy's fire.

The signal-guns broke the silence, the blaze of the second gun mingling in the smoke of the first, and salvoes rolled to the left and repeated themselves, the enemy's fine metal spreading its fire to the converging lines, ploughing the trembling ground, plunging through the line of batteries, and clouding the heavy air. The two or three hundred guns seemed proud of their undivided honors and organized confusion. The Confederates had the benefit of converging fire into the enemy's massed position, but the superior metal of the enemy neutralized the advantage of position. The brave and steady work progressed.

Major General Winfield S. Hancock as he rides along the Union lines during the Confederate bombardment prior to Pickett's Charge.

Less eager, but driven by honor and pride, were Pickett's brigade commanders, all of them older than Pickett, and all of them brigadier generals: Lewis A. Armistead, Richard B. Garnett, and James L. Kemper. Kemper was an eager secessionist who had been appointed for political reasons but had developed military skills; Armistead and Garnett were professionals with something to prove. Every generation of Virginia Armisteads since 1636 had fought in one of England's or America's wars. Lewis's father and four uncles had fought in the War of 1812. It must have been a matter of some family shame, therefore, when young Lewis was expelled from West Point in 1836, reportedly for hitting Jubal Early over the head with a dinner plate. Armistead went into the army anyway in 1839, and worked his way up to captain before resigning to join the Confederacy in 1861. One of his closest friends in the old army was Winfield Scott Hancock, who was waiting for him across the way as commander of the Union Second Corps holding the sector that the Confederates intended to attack.

"Up men, and to your posts! Don't forget today that you are from old Virginia."

Garnett had commanded the famed Stonewall Brigade under Stonewall Jackson in the battle of Kernstown in March 1862. When his men ran out of ammunition he had pulled them back. Jackson had him court-martialed for disobedience of orders and cowardice. Garnett was never tried, and was subsequently given a brigade under Pickett, but he felt the need to erase the stain on his honor. He was too ill to participate in this attack on foot, and was determined to lead his brigade on horseback, even though that would make him the prime target of every Union rifle within range. As Garnett and Armistead gazed across the fields at the blazing cannons on the ridge they were ordered to assault, Garnett commented, "This is a desperate thing to attempt." "It is," agreed Armistead. "But the issue is with the Almighty, and we must leave it in his hands."

Pickett's division would go forward on the right of the attacking line. We are standing about where the farthest right of Pettigrew's four brigades would start forward, with three more to the left and Trimble's brigades behind them. The whole line would be a mile wide when it emerged from the woods along Seminary Ridge, contracting to a width of only six hundred yards at the point of attack. Sometime between 2:00 and 3:00 PM (reports vary), Confederate batteries began to run short of ammunition. Longstreet's artillery commander, Colonel E. Porter Alexander, sent word that it was now or never for the infantry to go forward. "General," Pickett pleaded with Longstreet, "shall I advance?" Longstreet later wrote that "my feelings had so overcome me that I could not speak, for the fear of betraying my want of confidence." All he could do was nod. That was enough for Pickett. He rushed back to his men and gave them a short speech (which most could not hear), concluding, "Up men, and to your posts! Don't forget today that you are from old Virginia."

THE ORDER FOR THE CHARGE

By James Longstreet

Pickett said, "General, shall I advance?"

The effort to speak the order failed, and I could only indicate it by an affirmative bow. He accepted the duty with seeming confidence of success, leaped on his horse, and rode gayly to his command. I mounted and spurred for Alexander's post. He reported that the batteries he had reserved for the charge with the infantry had been spirited away by General Lee's chief of artillery; that the ammunition of the batteries of position was so reduced that he could not use them in proper support of the infantry. He was ordered to stop the march at once and fill up his ammunition-chests. But, alas! there was no more ammunition to be had.

Pickett taking his orders from Longstreet to charge.

The order was imperative. The Confederate commander had fixed his heart upon the work. Just then a number of the enemy's batteries hitched up and hauled off, which gave a glimpse of unexpected hope. Encouraging messages were sent for the columns to hurry on—and they were then on elastic springing step. The officers saluted as they passed, their stern smiles expressing confidence. General Pickett, a graceful horseman, sat lightly in the saddle, his brown locks flowing quite over his shoulders. Pettigrew's division spread their steps and quickly rectified the alignment, and the grand march moved bravely on. As soon as the leading columns opened the way, the supports sprang to their alignments. General Trimble mounted, adjusting his seat and reins with an air and grace as if setting out on a pleasant afternoon ride. When aligned to their places solid march was made down the slope and past our batteries of position.

General Gibbon's brigade driving back Pickett's Charge.

Forth they went, line after line. Almost as soon as they emerged from the woods near where we are standing, enemy artillery began to find the range. Confederate soldiers quickly learned that few if any Union cannons had been knocked out. Many of the times I have stood at this spot with a group of students, someone has asked me, "What made these men do it? What motivated them to advance into that wall of fire? What caused them to go forward despite the high odds against coming out unharmed?" The same questions could be asked about Union as well as Confederate soldiers on many a battlefield. I decided to write a book to answer the questions, using the letters and diaries of the soldiers themselves to find out what made them tick.

The answers to the questions are complex, as one might imagine, but they can be boiled down to the two motives expressed by the title of my book *For Cause and Comrades*. Most of the soldiers who fought at Gettysburg (and elsewhere) were volunteers. They had enlisted because they believed in the Cause (with a capital C) for which they were fighting: the very survival of their respective nations. If the North lost the war, the words "United States" would become an oxymoron. If the South lost, the Confederacy would exist no more. When the bullets started flying, however, the abstraction of Cause might fade into the background of the clear and present danger presented by those bullets. No sane person would walk alone for a thousand yards across open fields plowed by exploding shells, knowing that if he made it that far, grim men with rifles were waiting to shoot at him during the next three hundred yards. But if his comrades were going forward, he couldn't let them down by lagging behind. His fear of their contempt for his cowardice was greater than his fear of those shells and bullets. "You ask me if the thought of death does not alarm me," wrote one soldier to his sister. "I will say that I do not wish to die. . . . I myself am as big a coward as eny could be, but give me the bullet before the coward when all my friends and companions are going forward."

So, forward they went into a chaos of exploding shells that dropped men at almost every step. On they marched, closing ranks and keeping alignment almost as if they were on the parade ground. It was an awesome spectacle that participants on both sides remembered until the end of their lives—which for many came within the next half hour. We share that awe as we walk across these fields toward the Union line, hearing in our imagination the explosions of shells and the screams of the wounded.

As they approached the Union line, Pickett's division obliqued left so that the concentrated force of the attackers focused on that six-hundred-yard front. Yankee artillery and infantry waited behind their breastworks of fence rails and piled dirt and, for three hundred yards of that front, the protection of a stone wall. That wall made a ninety-degree turn to the east for sixty yards before resuming its south-north direction. As the attackers crossed the Emmitsburg Road, the spearhead of the assault headed toward that angle in the stone wall. Union artillery switched to canister (bullet-sized balls packed into casings), and Northern riflemen sent sheets of lead into those dense gray lines of infantry. On the right flank of Kemper's brigade, two Vermont regiments swung forward from the Union line and raked the Virginians with a devastating enfilading fire. Six hundred yards to the north, the Eighth Ohio did the same thing to Virginians and Mississippians in Pettigrew's division, aided by several companies of the 108th and 126th New York. The Ohioans deployed through the grounds of what was for decades the Home Sweet Home Motel. The National Park acquired this property in 2002 and razed the motel.

A collection of Confederate battle flags from the book **My Story of the War: A Woman's Narrative of Four Years Personal Experience as a Nurse in the Union Army** *by Mary Livermore.*

The nearest building now to the rear of the Eighth Ohio's position is General Pickett's Buffet and Battle Theater—which would amuse the Ohioans if they could come back.

In the face of these counterattacks, the Confederate flanks melted away like butter on a hot summer day. In the center, too, all was chaos. Longstreet's worst fears were coming true. Trimble went down with a wound that would cost him a leg. Pettigrew received a flesh wound in the hand. Garnett's riderless horse bolted out of the smoke; his master's body was later buried with his men and never identified. Kemper was crippled by a severe wound. All fifteen regimental commanders in Pickett's division went down; nine of them were killed. Thirteen of Pickett's regiments suffered the ignominy of having their flags captured by the enemy.

Perhaps two hundred men with Armistead had broken through the line at the angle in the stone wall, only to be shot down or captured by Union reserves who counterattacked to close

Pickett's Charge as seen from the Union lines.

A monument to the high-water mark of the Confederacy.

the breach. Armistead received a mortal wound as he placed his hand on an enemy cannon to claim its capture. By four o'clock it was all over. Unwounded but dazed Confederate survivors stumbled back to their starting point. Barely half returned. Of the forty-two regiments that took part in the primary attack, twenty-eight lost their colors to the enemy—by far the highest total for any one action in the war. In addition, of the eight supporting regiments that finally came forward—too late to help—one lost its flag as well.

A stroll around this "high water mark" of the Confederacy is well worth the time it takes to read the interpretive markers and absorb the information on the three dozen regimental monuments and the dozen or more tablets originally placed by the War Department. One Union monument in particular attracts our attention: the Seventy-second Pennsylvania monument with its bronze soldier atop a pedestal preparing to strike the enemy with his clubbed musket in hand-to-hand combat.

The Seventy-second was part of the Philadelphia brigade—four regiments from that city (69th, 71st, 72nd, and 106th Pennsylvania) which held the Union position that bore the brunt of the Confederate attack. The Seventy-second was originally in reserve about fifty yards to the rear of this monument (at a spot marked by an earlier regimental monument). When the veterans of the Seventy-second proposed in the 1880s to erect a second monument at the advanced position along the stone wall, the Gettysburg Battlefield Memorial Association refused permission. The veterans took the association to court. Several battle participants and witnesses testified for each side in this case. The brigade's commander, Brigadier General Alexander S. Webb, testified that at the crisis of the battle he had ordered the Seventy-second forward

The monument to the Seventy-second Pennsylvania.

Left: The marker showing wear Armistead fell, past the Union line.
Right: The position marker of the Eleventh Mississippi.

from its reserve position. They refused to go, he said. He tried to grab the national flag from the color sergeant to carry it forward, but the sergeant wouldn't let go. (Webb had been in command of the brigade for only a few days, so most of the men may not have known who he was.) Only after the enemy breakthrough had been contained and the assault repulsed, Webb claimed, did the regiment go forward to the place of honor where these craven cowards wanted to place their monument. Others disputed Webb's testimony, and in the end the judge ruled in favor of the Seventy-second's veterans. They got their second monument, on the front line. And perhaps they deserved it. Statistics of killed and wounded are a rough index of how hard a regiment fought. The Seventy-second had sixty-four killed and 125 wounded at Gettysburg—one-third of the brigade's casualties. It appears that they did quite a bit of fighting after all—or at least they took a lot of punishment.

Descendants of Confederates have had their own controversies about the placement of monuments at the high-water mark. That designation long belonged to the monument marking the spot where Armistead fell, about thirty yards on the Union side of the stone wall. But North Carolinians have disputed this placement of the high-water mark. They insist that a few men in the Twenty-sixth North Carolina penetrated twenty yards farther than the Virginian Armistead. Whatever the merits of this claim, the Twenty-sixth North Carolina unquestionably earned other distinctions. With a total of 840 men going into action on July 1, it was the largest regiment in either army. Its twenty-one-year-old "boy colonel," Henry Burgwyn, killed on July 1, was the youngest to hold that rank in either army. The regiment fought on both July 1 and 3, sustaining a total of 687 casualties, which was both the largest number and percentage (82 percent) for any regiment in the battle. (The same percentage in the First Minnesota on July 2 was for only eight of its ten companies.) Company F of the Twenty-sixth included four sets of twins, every one of whom was killed or wounded in the battle—a phenomenon unmatched by any other unit in the entire war.

Park historians accepted the claim that the Twenty-sixth advanced farther than any other regiment, and allowed North Carolina to place their monument at that point. But the place is to the north of the east-west jog of the stone wall, and outside the Union defensive line, while the Armistead monument represents a breakthrough of that line. The controversy reflects a long-standing dispute between Virginians and North Carolinians, who resented Virginia's domination of the writing of Confederate history. Much of the dispute has centered on "Pickett's Charge." North Carolinians maintain that it should be called "the Pickett-Pettigrew Charge" (Pettigrew was from North Carolina) because almost as many North Carolina regiments (fifteen) as Virginia regiments (nineteen) took part. And the Twenty-sixth North Carolina, they continue to insist, got farther than any Virginian. To assuage the bruised North Carolina ego, it is now politically correct to call it the Pickett-Pettigrew assault. But this in turn is misleading, for ten of those fifteen North Carolina regiments were in Trimble's two brigades, not in Pettigrew's division.

Having no choice, the lieutenant hoisted a white flag and surrendered to the Yankees of the 111th New York.

Not to be outdone, Mississippians have entered the fray. Under pressure from Senator Trent Lott of that state, the Park Service in 1998 allowed a monument to the Eleventh Mississippi to be placed about two hundred yards north of, and as close to the Union lines as, that of the Twenty-sixth North Carolina. The Eleventh Mississippi was a notable regiment. Most of its companies were composed of rough-hewn backwoodsmen, famous for their marksmanship. But all of the soldiers in Company A were University of Mississippi students who enlisted as a body in 1861—the University Greys. They later earned literary fame through the medium of William Faulkner's *Absalom, Absalom!* On July 3, 1863, a baker's dozen of the Eleventh did get as far as the place where their monument now stands. But what the tablet on the monument does not say is that when the lieutenant commanding this contingent looked back for the rest of the regiment, he was dismayed to see it running to the rear "in full disorder, at the distance of about one hundred & fifty yards from us." Having no choice, the lieutenant hoisted a white flag and surrendered to the Yankees of the 111th New York.

These controversies about who got the farthest would be amusing if Confederate heritage groups did not take the matter so seriously. Pickett's Charge—excuse me, the Pickett-Pettigrew assault—is viewed not only as the Confederacy's high-water mark, but also as one of the most courageous and praiseworthy events in military history. For decades the hearts of surviving veterans swelled with pride when they recounted their deeds in that attack. Southern honor knew no finer hour. I have always been struck by the contrast between this image and that of the Army of the Potomac's frontal assault against Confederate lines at Cold Harbor exactly eleven months later. In that attack, ordered by Lieutenant General Ulysses S. Grant, fifty thousand Union soldiers suffered seven thousand casualties, most of them in less than half an hour. For this mistake, which he admitted, Grant has been branded a "butcher" careless of the lives of his men, and Cold Harbor has become a symbol of mule-headed futility. At Gettysburg, Lee's men also sustained almost seven thousand casualties in the Pickett-Pettigrew assault, most of them also within a half hour. Yet this attack is perceived as an example of great courage and honor. This contrast speaks volumes about the comparative images of Grant and Lee, North and South, Union and Confederacy.

The Eleventh Mississippi monument stands close to the Brian house and barn. One of the park's markers spells the name as Bryan; the other, a few feet away, as Brian. Perhaps the Park Service agrees with Andrew Jackson, a notorious misspeller, who said that he could not respect any man who knew only one way to spell a word. In any case, Abraham Brian's twelve-acre farm was right smack in the middle of the fighting on July 3. Shells tore holes in his roof; bullets broke his windows; soldiers trampled his crops. But Brian/Bryan was not there to see it. Like many of the other 474 African Americans in Adams County—190 of them living in the town of Gettysburg—he had fled north with his family to put the Susquehanna River between them and the Confederates.

These black people had good reason to flee. Although most of them, including Brian and another black farmer who lived on the battlefield, James Warfield, had always been

The Brian house in July 1863.

African Americans were often called "contraband" by the Union during the war.

free, some were former slaves who had escaped from Maryland or Virginia. In the previous Confederate invasion of Union territory, in September 1862, Southern cavalry had made little distinction between free blacks and escaped slaves, driving dozens of them back to Virginia and slavery. They were doing the same thing again in Pennsylvania. In Chambersburg, two local residents wrote in their diaries that when Confederates entered the town in June, "one of the revolting features of this day was the scouring of the fields about the town and searching of houses in portions of the place for Negroes. . . . O! How it grated on our hearts to have to sit

"It's all my fault," he reportedly said. "It is I who have lost this fight, and you must help me out of it the best way you can. All good men must rally."

quietly & look at such brutal deeds—I saw no men among the contrabands—all women and children. Some of the colored people who were raised here were taken along."

The Chambersburg newspaper estimated that the rebels sent at least fifty local blacks back to Virginia. A diarist raised the estimate to 250 from Franklin County. Blacks in Gettysburg had plenty of warning, and cleared out. Some never returned. Abraham Brian did return. He repaired his house and tided his family over until the next season by exhuming the bodies of Union soldiers at a dollar each for reinterment in the soldiers' cemetery dedicated in November. Brian submitted a claim of more than a thousand dollars to the federal government for damages to his farm. He received forty-five dollars.

As the walking wounded and unwounded survivors of the Pickett-Pettigrew attack reached their own lines, they found Lee and Longstreet working vigorously to patch together a defense against an expected counterattack. "General Pickett," said Lee to a slumped figure from whom all thoughts of glory had fled, "place your division in the rear of this hill, and be ready to repel the advance of the enemy should they follow up their advantage." "General Lee," replied Pickett despairingly, "I have no division now." According to later recollections by Confederate soldiers, Lee rode among his men to buck up their spirits. "It's all my fault," he reportedly said. "It is I who have lost this fight, and you must help me out of it the best way you can. All good men must rally."

Shown here after his risky victory at Chancellorsville, Lee was well loved by his men and could rally them to seemingly any cause.

REFLECTIONS ON GETTYSBURG

ON LEE'S RESPONSE TO THE BATTLE

From: Colonel T. J. Goree
To: James Longstreet

I was present, however, just after Pickett's repulse, when General Lee so magnanimously took all the blame of the disaster upon himself. Another important circumstance, which I distinctly remember, was in the winter of 1863–64, when you sent me from East Tennessee to Orange Court-House with some despatches to General Lee. Upon my arrival there, General Lee asked me into his tent, where he was alone, with two or three Northern papers on the table. He remarked that he had just been reading the Northern reports of the battle of Gettysburg; that he had become satisfied from reading those reports that if he had permitted you to carry out your plan, instead of making the attack on Cemetery Hill, he would have been successful.

◇◇◇◇◇◇◇◇◇◇◇◇◇

Harper's Weekly *was the most widely read Northern paper during the Civil War.*

FROM BERRYVILLE, CLARKE COUNTY, VIRGINIA, 1868

From: Robert E. Lee
To: Major Wm. M. McDonald

As to the battle of Gettysburg, I must again refer you to the official accounts. Its loss was occasioned by a combination of circumstances. It was commenced in the absence of correct intelligence. It was continued in the effort to overcome the difficulties by which we were surrounded, and it would have been gained could one determined and united blow have been delivered by our whole line. As it was, victory trembled in the balance for three days, and the battle resulted in the infliction of as great an amount of injury as was received and in frustrating the Federal campaign for the season.

★ ★ ★

A Currier & Ives lithograph depicting battle on July 3.

Rally they did, after a fashion. But Meade did not order a counterattack. It was not for lack of urging by at least some of his subordinates, including Hancock. Wounded at the height of the action by a bullet that drove a bent nail from his saddle into his thigh, Hancock—misinterpreting the source of the nail—said, "They must be hard up for ammunition if they throw such a shot as that."

The Confederates *were* short of artillery ammunition. And they had lost at least 23,000—perhaps as many as 28,000—killed, wounded, and captured men during these three days. But Meade, who knew that his own army had been hurt—23,000 casualties altogether—could not know just how badly off his adversary was. The Union commander's failure to follow up his victory with a counterthrust during the nearly four hours of remaining daylight on July 3 provoked criticism at the time and through the years. He had kept the 13,000 fresh troops of the Sixth Corps in reserve; most of them had not fired a shot in the battle. Eight thousand of them were on alert a mile south of the area where the heaviest fighting took place, but Meade had not sent word for them to deploy, nor did he do so after the Confederates were repulsed.

Meade has his defenders, however. They point out that a heavy load of responsibility weighed on his shoulders. He had been in command for only six days, three of them fighting for his army's survival. Could he jeopardize his victory by risking a counterattack against an enemy that still had sharp teeth and might bite back as hard as it had been bitten? "We have done well enough," said Meade to a cavalry officer eager to do more. Meade later explained that he did not want to follow "the bad example [Lee] had set me, in ruining himself attacking a strong position."

Out on the Union left flank more than two miles south of Meade's headquarters, however, one Union officer anticipated an order for a counterattack. He was Brigadier General Judson

General Judson Kilpatrick.

Kilpatrick, commander of a Union cavalry division. Learning at about 5:00 PM of the repulse of the Pickett-Pettigrew assault, Kilpatrick ordered a combined mounted and dismounted attack by two brigades against the Confederate right flank west of the Round Tops. Unsupported by infantry, this attack was a bloody fiasco. From a point near the monument to Major William Wells of the First Vermont Cavalry on South Confederate Avenue, we can view the scenes of the mounted attack through the fields of the Slyder farm. Before the Park Service cleared out twenty-seven acres of woods west of the Slyder farmhouse that were not there in 1863, and before a hundred-acre woodlot south of the road was culled, it was impossible to visualize how cavalry could operate in this area. Now, happily, we can understand the tactics of Kilpatrick's attack—faulty and foolhardy though it proved to be.

Next day—the Fourth of July—Union infantry from the Fifth and Sixth Corps moved out from the vicinity of the Round Tops to probe Confederate positions in that area. Was this the beginning of a Union counterattack? Impossible to say, for in late morning a drenching rain began to fall and continued intermittently for several days, bringing operations to a halt. Lee had already decided to retreat, and that evening his army started to pull out and head for Virginia. The rain hindered both the retreat and Meade's snaillike pursuit.

Heavy rain fell after several Civil War battles. A widespread theory at the time held that the thunder of artillery somehow caused clouds to let loose their own thunder and moisture. I am unable to say whether this theory holds water.

Rain coming in over the hills of Gettysburg.

MEADE'S THANKS TO THE ARMY OF THE POTOMAC

GENERAL ORDERS, NO. 68, FROM MEADE

The Commanding General, in behalf of the country, thanks the Army of the Potomac for the glorious result of the recent operations.

An enemy superior in numbers and flushed with the pride of a successful invasion, attempted to overcome and destroy this Army. Utterly baffled and defeated, he has now withdrawn from the contest. The privations and fatigue the Army has endured, and the heroic courage and gallantry it has displayed will be matters of history to be remembered.

Our task is not yet accomplished, and the Commanding General looks to the Army for greater efforts to drive from our soil every vestige of the presence of the invader.

It is right and proper that we should, on all suitable occasions, return our grateful thanks to the Almighty Disposer of events, that in the goodness of His Providence He has thought fit to give victory to the cause of the just.

★ ★ ★

The monument to General Meade at Gettysburg.

EPILOGUE

THE CONFEDERATE retreat from Gettysburg turned into a nightmare. An ambulance train several miles long jounced over rutted roads and bogged down axle-deep in mud, causing untold agony for the ten thousand wounded men that the Army of Northern Virginia managed to take along on the retreat. They had to leave behind at least seven thousand wounded to be treated by Union surgeons, who had their hands full with fourteen thousand Union wounded. As well as farmhouses and barns on the battlefield, virtually every public building and many homes in town became hospitals. The medical corps set up numerous tent hospitals as well. Hundreds of volunteers flocked to Gettysburg to help care for the wounded. Burial details hastily interred more than three thousand dead Union soldiers and many of the almost four thousand dead Confederates. Four thousand of the wounded, about evenly divided between the two sides, subsequently died of their wounds. Five thousand dead horses were doused with coal oil and burned. For months the stench of hospitals, and of corpses unburied or buried in shallow graves, hung over the town and countryside.

Meanwhile the Army of the Potomac, prodded by President Lincoln and General-in-Chief Halleck, plodded through the mud in pursuit of Lee. Union cavalry captured the Confederate wagon train carrying the pontoons necessary to bridge the Potomac. Swollen by rain, the river was unfordable. Lincoln urged Meade to attack the rebels while they were trapped north of the Potomac. Lee fortified a

An ambulance train at City Point, Virginia.

ANNOUNCEMENT OF THE VICTORY AT GETTYSBURG

FROM PRESIDENT ABRAM LINCOLN AT THE WAR DEPARTMENT

July 4, 10:30 AM

The President announces to the country that news from the Army of the Potomac, up to 10 PM of the 3rd, is such as to cover that army with the highest honor, to promise a great success to the cause of the Union, and to claim the condolence of all for the many gallant fallen; and that for this he especially desires that on this day He whose will, not ours, should ever be done be everywhere remembered and reverenced with profoundest gratitude.

★ ★ ★

This portrait of Lincoln hangs at the Blair House, located across from the White House.

defensive perimeter at Williamsport, Maryland (forty miles southwest of Gettysburg), with both flanks on the river. There he awaited attack while his engineer corps frantically tore down buildings to construct a new set of pontoons to bridge the raging Potomac.

When news reached Washington of Vicksburg's surrender to Grant on the Fourth of July, and of other Union victories in Tennessee and Louisiana, Lincoln was jubilant. "If General Meade can complete his work by the literal or substantial destruction of Lee's army," said the Union president on July 7, "the rebellion will be over." Lincoln hovered around the War Department telegraph office "anxious and impatient" for news from Meade. But the Union commander and his men were exhausted from lack of sleep and endless slogging through quagmires called roads. The Confederate earthworks at Williamsport were formidable, even though Lee had only 45,000 tired men to defend them while reinforcements had brought Meade's strength back up to 85,000. Meade's famous temper grew short as messages from Halleck pressed him to attack. Lincoln's temper also grew short. When Meade finally telegraphed on July 12 that he intended "to attack them tomorrow, unless something intervenes," Lincoln commented acidly, "They will be ready to fight a magnificent battle when there is no enemy to fight."

Edwin Forbes's Last Stand of the Army of Virginia *shows Lee's defensive line at the Potomac.*

GRANT ON THE VICTORY OF VICKSBURG

GENERAL GRANT'S REPORT TO GENERAL-IN-CHIEF HALLECK

"The enemy surrendered this morning. The only terms allowed is their parole as prisoners of war. This I regard as a great advantage to us at this moment. It saves, probably, several days in the capture, and leaves troops and transports ready for immediate service. Sherman, with a large force, moves immediately on Johnston, to drive him from the State. I will send troops to the relief of Banks, and return the 9th army corps to Burnside."

★ ★ ★

A Kurz & Allison lithograph of the Siege of Vicksburg, showing General Grant looking through a field glass.

GRANT RECALLS DUAL VICTORIES

FROM THE PERSONAL MEMOIRS OF ULYSSES S. GRANT

This news, with the victory at Gettysburg won the same day, lifted a great load of anxiety from the minds of the President, his Cabinet and the loyal people all over the North. The fate of the Confederacy was sealed when Vicksburg fell. Much hard fighting was to be done afterwards and many precious lives were to be sacrificed; but the morale was with the supporters of the Union ever after.

A portrait of Grant by Mathew Brady.

In this painting by Forbes, Lee's army crosses the Potomac River at night.

Events proved Lincoln right. Meade delayed another day, and when the Army of the Potomac went forward on July 14 they found nothing but a rear guard. The dropping river had enabled the enemy to vanish across a patched-together bridge and a nearby ford during the night. "Great God!" exclaimed Lincoln when he heard this news. "We had them in our grasp. We had only to stretch forth our hands and they were ours. Our army held the war in the hollow of their hand and would not close it."

Lincoln may have been right about that—or he may not have been. A Union assault might have succeeded—with heavy casualties—or it might not have.

In either case, destruction of Lee's veteran army was far from a certainty. When Meade learned of Lincoln's dissatisfaction, he offered his resignation. This was a serious matter. Despite his caution and slowness, Meade had won public acclaim for his victory at Gettysburg. Lincoln could hardly afford to fire him two weeks after the battle. So he refused to accept the resignation, and sat down to write Meade a soothing letter.

As the president's pen scratched across the paper, however, the letter became anything but soothing. Gettysburg was a "magnificent success" for which Lincoln was "very—very—grateful to you." But, "my dear General," the president continued, "I do not believe you appreciate the magnitude of the misfortune involved in Lee's escape. He was within your easy grasp, and to have closed upon him would, in connection with our other late successes, have ended the war. As it is, the war will be prolonged indefinitely. Your golden opportunity is gone, and I am distressed immeasurably because of it." As Lincoln reread these words, he realized that the letter would scarcely mollify Meade's feelings. So he filed it away in his papers and never sent it.

Page one of Lincoln's four-page letter to Meade.

The war did continue for another twenty-one months. Whether it would have ended if Meade had "closed upon" Lee at Williamsport is anybody's guess. In any event, people in the North immediately saw Gettysburg as a turning point in their favor. "VICTORY WATERLOO ECLIPSED!" blazoned the headline in a Philadelphia newspaper. In New York a lawyer wrote in his diary that "the results of this victory are priceless. The charm of Robert Lee's invincibility is broken. The Army of the Potomac has at last found a general that can handle it, and has stood nobly up to its terrible work in spite of its long disheartening list of hard-fought failures. Copperheads are palsied and dumb for the moment at least. Government is strengthened four-fold at home and abroad."

In London the news of Gettysburg and Vicksburg drove the final nail into the coffin of Confederate hopes for European diplomatic recognition. "The disasters of the rebels are unre-deemed by even any hope of success," wrote young Henry Adams from London, where he was secretary to his father, the American minister to the Court of St. James. "It is now conceded that all idea of [British] intervention is at an end."

Some southerners also recognized the pivotal importance of Gettysburg. "The news from Lee's army is appalling," wrote Confederate War Department clerk John B. Jones in his diary

LEE'S SON CAPTURED AND THE RETREAT FROM THE NORTH

FROM WILLIAMSPORT, TO HIS WIFE, MARY CUSTIS LEE

I have heard with great grief that Fitzhugh has been captured by the enemy. Had not expected that he would be taken from his bed and carried off, but we must bear this additional affliction with fortitude and resignation, and not repine at the will of God. It will eventuate in some good that we know not of now. We must bear our labours and hardships manfully. Our noble men are cheerful and confident. I constantly remember you in my thoughts and prayers.

<><><><><><><><><>

FROM NEAR HAGERSTOWN

The consequences of war are horrid enough at best, surrounded by all the ameliorations of civilisation and Christianity. I am very sorry for the injuries done the family at Hickory Hill, and particularly that our dear old Uncle Williams, in his eightieth year, should be subjected to such treatment. But we cannot help it, and must endure it. You will, however, learn before this reaches you that our success at Gettysburg was not so great as reported—in fact, that we failed to drive the enemy from his position, and that our army withdrew to the Potomac. Had the river not unexpectedly risen, all would have been well with us; but God, in His all-wise providence, willed otherwise, and our communications have been interrupted and almost cut off. The waters have subsided to about four feet, and, if they continue, by to-morrow, I hope, our communications will be open. I trust that a merciful God, our only hope and refuge, will not desert us in this hour of need, and will deliver us by His almighty hand, that the whole world may recognise His power and all hearts be lifted

Robert E. Lee and his son William photographed fifteen years before the start of the Civil War.

up in adoration and praise of His unbounded loving-kindness. We must, however, submit to His almighty will, whatever that may be. May God guide and protect us all is my constant prayer.

An 1864 printing of the Emancipation Proclamation.

on July 9. "This is the darkest day of the war." The fire-eating Virginia secessionist Edmund Ruffin "never before felt so despondent as to our struggle." Confederate Ordnance Chief Josiah Gorgas, who had performed miracles to keep Southern armies supplied with weapons and ammunition, wrote in his diary at the end of July 1863: "Events have succeeded one another with disastrous rapidity. One brief month ago we were apparently at the point of success. Lee was in Pennsylvania, threatening Harrisburg, and even Philadelphia, Vicksburg seemed to laugh all Grant's efforts to scorn. . . . It seems incredible that human power could effect such a change in so brief a space. Yesterday

Soldiers' National Cemetery in 1903.

we rode on the pinnacle of success—today absolute ruin seems to be our portion." By this time Lincoln had recovered his spirits. In early August his private secretary wrote that the president "is in fine whack. I have seldom seen him so serene." In addition to other Union military successes that took place in the latter half of 1863, the administration's emancipation policy gained broader support in the North. The Union army began organizing black regiments composed mainly of former slaves. They acquitted themselves well in minor battles during 1863. The off-year state elections of 1863, especially in the key states of Pennsylvania and Ohio, were shaping up as a sort of referendum on the Emancipation Proclamation. Republicans won impressive victories in those elections. If the Emancipation Proclamation had been submitted to a referendum a year earlier, commented an Illinois newspaper in November, "there is little doubt that the voice of a majority would have been against it. And not a year has passed before it is approved by an overwhelming majority." A New Yorker noted that "the change of opinion on this slavery question since 1860 is a great historical fact. God pardon our blindness of three years ago."

No single event did more to change the Northern mood than the victory at Gettysburg. It was appropriate, therefore, that Lincoln should offer the most profound and eloquent statement there on the meaning of this new birth of freedom.

Soon after the battle, David Wills, a Gettysburg lawyer, proposed to Governor Andrew Curtin of Pennsylvania the establishment of a soldiers' cemetery where the Union dead could be reburied with dignity and honor. Curtin contacted the governors of other Northern states whose soldiers had died at Gettysburg. They all thought it was a splendid idea. The project went forward, and became the model for reinterment of Union war dead in two dozen national cemeteries during and after the war. (Many Confederate dead were reburied in Confederate cemeteries throughout the South.) The dedication of the soldiers' cemetery at Gettysburg adjacent

This 1867 New York print of the Battle of Gettysburg reinforced the widely held opinion that this battle was a turning point.

CONTINUED FAILURE TO PURSUE THE ENEMY

A TELEGRAM TO GENERAL H. W. HALLECK SENT FROM SOLDIERS' HOME, WASHINGTON, JULY 6, 1863

Major-General Halleck:

I left the telegraph office a good deal dissatisfied. You know I did not like the phrase—in Orders, No. 68, I believe—"Drive the invaders from our soil." Since that, I see a despatch from General French, saying the enemy is crossing his wounded over the river in flats, without saying why he does not stop it, or even intimating a thought that it ought to be stopped. Still later, another despatch from General Pleasonton, by direction of General Meade, to General French, stating that the main army is halted because it is believed the rebels are concentrating "on the road towards Hagerstown, beyond Fairfield," and is not to move until it is ascertained that the rebels intend to evacuate Cumberland Valley.

These things appear to me to be connected with a purpose to cover Baltimore and Washington and to get the enemy across the river again without a further collision, and they do not appear connected with a

General H. W. Halleck.

purpose to prevent his crossing and to destroy him. I do fear the former purpose is acted upon and the latter rejected.

If you are satisfied the latter purpose is entertained, and is judiciously pursued, I am content. If you are not so satisfied, please look to it.

Yours truly,
Abraham Lincoln

★ ★ ★

to the local burial ground where some of the fighting had taken place, occurred on November 19, 1863.

Let us conclude our walk by proceeding to this most hallowed of ground, where some 3,577 Union soldiers (half of them unknown) from eighteen states are buried. None of them was from Kentucky. But at the spot where Lincoln was long thought to have stood to deliver his "few appropriate remarks," Kentucky erected a modest marker to her native son, enshrining in bronze the 272 words of the address Lincoln delivered that day. (The actual spot was probably thirty yards to the south, but it hardly matters.) Edward Everett, the main orator of the occasion, penned Lincoln a note next day: "I should be glad, if I could flatter myself that I came as near to the central idea of the occasion, in two hours, as you did in two minutes."

It is best to come here at dusk, as I do when I take students to Gettysburg, and listen to the call of mourning doves as we look out over the graves in this pastoral setting. It is then that we contemplate the real meaning of "that cause for which they gave the last full measure of devotion." Gettysburg is important not primarily as the high-water mark of the Confederacy, but as the place where "this nation, under God, shall have a new birth of freedom."

The Gettysburg Address monument.

President Abraham Lincoln's Address at the Dedication of the Soldiers' Cemetery in Gettysburg November 19, 1863

Four score and seven years ago our fathers brought forth on this continent, a new nation, conceived in Liberty, and dedicated to the proposition that all men are created equal.

Now we are engaged in a great civil war, testing whether that nation, or any nation so conceived and so dedicated, can long endure. We are met on a great battle-field of that war. We have come to dedicate a portion of that field, as a final resting place for those who here gave their lives that the nation might live. It is altogether fitting and proper that we should do this.

But, in a larger sense, we can not dedicate—we can not consecrate—we can not hallow—this ground. The brave men, living and dead, who struggled here, have consecrated it, far above our poor power to add or detract. The world will little note, nor long remember what we say here, but it can never forget what they did here. It is for us the living, rather, to be dedicated here to the unfinished work which they who fought here have thus far so nobly advanced. It is rather for us to be here dedicated to the great task remaining before us—that from these honored dead we take increased devotion to that cause for which they gave the last full measure of devotion—that we here highly resolve that these dead shall not have died in vain—that this nation, under God, shall have a new birth of freedom—and that government of the people, by the people, for the people, shall not perish from the earth.

Top: The original, handwritten Gettysburg Address. Bottom: In this photograph of the stage at the dedication ceremony where Lincoln gave the Gettysburg Address, the president is visible about an inch below the flag, three men over to the right. He is hatless and his head is slightly bowed.

IMAGE CREDITS

pp. iv–v, viii–ix, x–xi, (bottom), xvi–1, 2, 5, 6, 7, 8–9, 10, 11 (all), 12–13, 14–15, 19, 25, 28, 31, 32–33, 35, 37, 39, 40, 41, 42, 43 (bottom), 47 (all), 48–49, 52, 53, 58, 59, 62–63, 65, 66, 72, 73, 74, 79, 82–83, 88–89, 90, 92–93, 94–95, 96, 97, 104, 106–107, 111, 120, 125, 126–127, 128 (top), 129, 132, 134–135, 137, 138–139, 140–141, 143, 145, 146, 156, 157 (left), 159, 160–161, 163, 166–167, 172–173, 174, 175, 178, 184–185, 186, 187, 188, 189, 190, 191, 194, 195, 196–197, 198, 203 (bottom) courtesy of the Library of Congress; p. vi © Andrew McDonough/Shutterstock; p. x (top) by photographer Buddy Secor, courtesy of the National Park Service; pp. xi (top), xii, 4, 17, 157 (right) courtesy of the Internet Book Archive/flickr; p. xiii © Michael M.S./flickr; pp. xiv–xv © Bo Gordy-Stith; pp. 3, 22, 77, 98, 109, 131, 150 by Hal Jespersen; p. 16 © Lpockras; p. 23 © justasc/Shutterstock; p. 24 © Mr.TinDC/flickr; pp. 26–27, 153 © Rob Shenk/flickr; pp. 29, 87, 142, 170 (right) © Ron Cogswell/flickr; pp. 34 (top), 44 courtesy of the National Park Service; p. 34 (bottom left) courtesy of Don Wiles; p. 34 (bottom right) © Ray Fincham Sr.; p. 43 (top), 56, 95, 96, 128 (bottom), 133, 165, courtesy of Wikimedia Commons; p. 45 © Carptrash/Wikimedia Commons; pp. 46, 80 (left) © fauxto_digit/flirckr; p. 50 courtesy of MilitaryHealth/flickr; p. 52 Courtesy of the National Library of Medicine; p. 55 © steve estvanik/Shutterstock; p. 61 courtesy of the Texas State Library Archives and Commission; pp. 68–69 © Adam Parent/Shutterstock; pp. 70–71 by Don Troiani, Courtesy of the National Guard; p. 75 and endpaper map reproduction courtesy of the Norman B. Leventhal Map Center at the Boston Public Library; p. 76 courtesy of the West Point Museum Collection, United States Military Academy; pp. 78, 124 courtesy of The Tichnor Brothers Collection, Boston Public Library, Print Department; p. 80 (right) ©keithreifsnyder/flickr; p. 81 © Acroterion/Wikimedia Commons; p. 83 © Chris Favero/flickr; pp. 84, 91 © keithreifsnyder/flickr; p. 84 © Jon Dawson/flickr; p. 99 © Pable Sanchez/flickr; p. 101 © Espino Family/flickr; p. 103 © Matthew T. Bradley/flickr; p. 105 © Bo Gordy-Stith/Wikimedia Commons; p. 114 © AppalachianViews/iStock; pp. 117, 162 © IADA/Shutterstsock; pp. 118–119 courtesy of the National Guard; p. 121 © Samuel Murray/Wikimedia Commons; pp. 122, 171 © blue-67sign/Shutterstock; p. 123 courtesy of Donaldecoho/Wikimedia Commons; p. 136 © m01229/flickr; p. 144 Courtesy of Adams County Historical Society; p. 147 © catnap72 / iStock; pp. 148–149 © Lance Neilson/flickr; p. 151 © jemartin03/flickr; p. 152 © David W Crippen/Shutterstock; p. 155 © Condor 36/Shutterstock; p. 157 © Denton Rumsey/Shutterstock; p. 158 © Colin Baxter/flickr; p. 164 Courtesy of the Stephen A. Schwarzman Building/Photography Collection, Miriam and Ira D. Wallach Division of Art, Prints and Photographs/Wikimedia Commons; p. 168 © Harvey Barrison/flickr; p. 169 Courtesy of Smallbones/Wikimedia; p. 170 © Frank Kovalchek/flickr; p. 177 © Konstantin L/Shutterstock; p. 179 courtesy of the National Archives; pp. 180–181 © C. Kurt Holter/Shutterstock; p. 183 © Carolyn/flickr; p. 192 courtesy of the Virginia Historical Society/Wikimedia Commons; pp. 199–200 © Jeremy R. Smith Sr./Shutterstock; p. 203 courtesy of ourdocuments.gov/National Archives and Records Administration.

INDEX

Note: Page numbers in *italics* indicate photographs, artwork, and maps.

ABOUT THE AUTHOR

James M. McPherson was born in North Dakota and grew up in Minnesota, where he graduated from Gustavus Adolphus College. He did his graduate study at the Johns Hopkins University in Baltimore, where he became fascinated by the American Civil War and the issues over which it was fought. While in graduate school he began visiting Civil War battlefields, including Gettysburg. During forty years on the faculty at Princeton University, he has taken students, colleagues, alumni, and many other groups on tours of the Gettysburg battlefield on numerous occasions. *Hallowed Ground* is his fourteenth book on the Civil War era. His *Battle Cry of Freedom: The Civil War Era* (1988) won the Pulitzer Prize for history in 1989, and his *For Cause and Comrades* (1997) won the Lincoln Prize in 1998. He is currently serving as president of the American Historical Association.

Brimming with creative inspiration, how-to projects, and useful information to enrich your everyday life, Quarto Knows is a favorite destination for those pursuing their interests and passions. Visit our site and dig deeper with our books into your area of interest: Quarto Creates, Quarto Cooks, Quarto Homes, Quarto Lives, Quarto Drives, Quarto Explores, Quarto Gifts, or Quarto Kids.

This edition published in 2017 by Crestline
an imprint of The Quarto Group
142 West 36th St, 4th Floor
New York, NY 10018

Published by Zenith Press
Acquisitions Editor: Erik Gilg
Project Manager: Madeleine Vasaly
Art Director: James Kegley

Created by Warren Street Books
Editorial Director: Carlo DeVito
Editor: Katherine Furman
Designer: Ashley Prine

ISBN-13: 978-0-7858-3560-8

Back flap photo by David K. Crow, courtesy of the author.

Front cover photo title: The Battle of Gettysburg / P.F. Rothermel
Repository: Library of Congress Prints and Photographs Division, Washington, D.C. 20540 USA

Printed in China

10 9 8 7 6 5 4 3 2 1